A WOMAN'S BOOK OF PRAYERS

Rita F. Snowden is widely known in many countries and is the author of more than sixty books for adults and children. After six years at business she trained as a deaconess of the New Zealand Methodist Church, serving in turn two pioneer country areas before moving to the largest city for several years of social work during an economic depression.

Miss Snowden has served the world Church, beyond her own denomination, with regular broadcasting commitments. She has written and spoken in Britain, Canada, the United States, in Australia, and in Tonga at the invitation of Queen Salote. She has represented her church at the World Methodist Conference at Oxford; later being elected the first woman Vice-President of the New Zealand Methodist Church, and President of its Deaconess Association. She is an Honorary Vice-President of the New Zealand Women Writers' Society, a Fellow of the International Institute of Art and Letters, and a member of P.E.N.

Miss Snowden has been honoured by the award of the Order of the British Empire, and by the citation of "The Upper Room" in America.

Her most recent books include *Bedtime Stories and Prayers* (for children), *I Believe Here and Now*, *Discoveries That Delight*, *Further Good News*, *Continually Aware*, *Good Company*, *Prayers in Large Print*, *Like Wind on the Grasses*, *Secrets* and *A Good Harvest*.

D0774437

*Books by the same author
available in Fount Paperbacks*

Christmas – And Always
More Prayers for Women
Secrets
Sharing Surprises

Rita Snowden also edited
In the Hands of God
by William Barclay

RITA F. SNOWDEN

A Woman's Book of Prayers

foreword by
WILLIAM BARCLAY

Fount
An Imprint of HarperCollins*Publishers*

Fount Paperbacks is an Imprint of
HarperCollins*Religious*
Part of HarperCollins*Publishers*
77–85 Fulham Palace Road,
Hammersmith, London W6 8JB

First published in Great Britain
in 1968 by Fount Paperbacks
23 25 27 29 30 28 26 24

A catalogue record for this book is
available from the British Library

ISBN 0 00 623685 5

Set in Garamond

Printed in Great Britain by
HarperCollinsManufacturing Glasgow

FOREWORD

I have read Miss Snowden's prayers for the present-day woman with very great interest. It seems to me to answer almost perfectly to its title. The language is modern and yet the language is beautiful. A pattern of prayer is kept all the way through, but what seems to me most important of all is this—there is all through the book an accent of reality. It prays for things which people really want. It thinks in situations which are happening to everyone. It takes the life of every day and lays it before God. And this is precisely what a book like this should do. I am quite sure that this book will make prayer more real and meaningful for all who use it. Here the needs of the twentieth century are brought to God in twentieth century language and the everlasting needs are also laid before the throne of grace.

WILLIAM BARCLAY

CONTENTS

Preface 9

Prayers with Bible Readings
for Thirty Days 13

Prayers with Bible Readings
for Five Sundays 77

Six Graces for Use at Table 89

Prayers with Bible Readings
for Festival Days 91

Prayers for Special Occasions
and Particular Occupations 107

PREFACE

Prayer to a present-day woman is as natural as breathing—not because she is specially holy, but because she is a human being.

Stand beside the one dearest to you, and together watch a new day's sun come up behind grape-blue hills, and see if it is not so; tear open a telegram carrying good news, after a time of deep anxiety, and see if it is not so; stand beside the hospital bed of a little child, when the last modern drug has failed, and see if it is not so. Ecstasy, thankfulness, need, are but a few of life's experiences that lead a woman to pray.

Prayer rises like this, when our inmost being speaks; we are made that way. It wouldn't happen to a family pet, a horse, a cat, a dog, but it always happens to men and women, whether spoken outwardly or not, wherever life sets them down—out in the desert beneath wide skies, under a biblical tent of camel's hair, in a city tenement up worn stairs, in a new house in the country, in a flat in town, or in a skyscraper with its head in the clouds. A cooking-bar between two stones, a wooden safe on the shady side, wall-to-wall carpets—it makes no difference.

The words Jesus spoke when life was young are still relevant: giving his close friends what we call 'The Lord's Prayer', he did not say, 'If you pray . . . set about it like this,' he said, 'When you pray. . . .' For there was to him no doubt that they would pray. The time would come—though it might wait for a crisis—when they would pray as naturally as they reached out for something solid when falling. That was what kindly-wise George Herbert meant in a simpler century than yours and mine, when he said: 'He that will learn to pray, let him go to sea.' That must have had more meaning in that day of sailing ships. In our day, I shall never forget when I prayed in a howling cyclone, my cabin timbers creaking mercilessly. Others of us as urgently prayed when bombs were falling, and a beloved city was burning.

William James, the distinguished philosopher, sums it up,

when he says : ' Many reasons have been given why we should not pray, whilst others are given why we should. But in all this very little is said of the reason why we do pray. The reason why we pray is simply that we cannot help praying.'

The pity is, that for many women it is only a crisis experience. The rest of the time, some of us seem to think we can get along quite nicely without it. Why is this? There are surely a number of reasons. First, we ought to ask, perhaps, what prayer really is—beyond being delivered from a situation plainly beyond our powers. Most days go along smoothly enough—we manage.

This is to ignore the greatest thing about prayer—that it is much more than just getting things. It is fellowship with God, who created us, and cared for us before ever we were born, and set us each down here as a member of his earthly family. From him, and no other, we have received this swift and wonderful trust of life. Communion with him, here and now, is at the very heart of prayer. It is a family relationship—an earthly child, communing with the heavenly Father, who is holy love. Stumbling to put it into words, one has said : ' It is lifting up one's eyes to the hills and knowing their strength and one's littleness . . . It is like going into a place so clean that one draws back lest he soil that cleanness. It is like standing in a light before which one must shade one's eyes. It is like hearing a rebuke from one you love, and knowing it is true, and feeling inwardly smitten. It is like receiving a gift beyond all expectation, and not knowing what to say . . . It is like all these, but it is not the same as any of these.'

You might like to add, out of your experience, it is richness of love and understanding so real that I am able to speak my inmost thoughts, my hidden desires, my hopes, my fears, holding nothing back. And, you might want to add, I get this confidence because Jesus talked to God like this, right up to his dying moments on the Cross. ' Father, into Your hands I commend my spirit,' he said. So God was Father still—even there. And there is no conceivable situation when he won't be that to me—though my wild-headedness take me into the far country. Jesus told of a father's eyes shaded against the light, picking out a tiny distant whirl of dust raised by the feet of one he missed terribly, long before the prodigal could stumble into his arms or mutter his shame in a little speech he had made up. That is the sort of divine father of our spirits, to whom we pray.

If this were possible only once or twice in our lives, how we would value that privilege! If we could avail ourselves of this experience we call prayer, only in a special place to which few could go, how we would scrape and save, counting no economy or inconvenience too much.

If we always got exactly what we asked for—and not, in God's long-sighted loving purpose, something better—we might, perhaps, give more attention to prayer. We are so 'thing-minded', so set on our material wants, our own brief purposes.

If we could get bread for our families only by approaching the God of Harvest with the words 'Give us this day our daily bread . . .' and not for a few pence over the counter at the corner store, we might, perhaps, give prayer a larger place in our lives. But clearly, this petition involves the use of the best seed, agricultural tools, and methods of distribution by the world's merchants. Yet it is more personal than that—it is bound up with the money we spend, the meals that come daily to our own tables, and with the food we throw away. Bread matters everywhere so much—because in the Father's world people matter so much.

If we didn't feel so decent, so materially secure, so smug, perhaps, we might more readily pray 'forgive us as we forgive', since forgiveness is the only key that fits the family life of this world and the granting of forgiveness is conditioned by forgiveness offered. Forgiveness is always much more than a penalty remitted—it is a relationship restored.

If one was not so busy looking after the house, standing in the shopping queue, getting the meals, and making sure one has something to wear, one might more easily, perhaps, be aware of being a whole personality—with body, mind, and spirit. But the older one grows, the busier one seems to get—so many more people come into one's life, so many more interests lay claim to one's attention! For it takes time to pray—though one can pray anywhere, at any time.

And one doesn't need to commit to memory particular words, stately, high-sounding phrases from the past. Prayer being as natural as breathing, one can pray in everyday words—and about everyday things. Though some women, in the midst of this modern life we share—like Rose

Macaulay the novelist—seem to find help in the traditional prayers of the Church, and collect them for use, they may appear archaic to others. Some pray best kneeling; some like to stand. Others, seeking the most helpful posture, relax in a chair so that they don't have to think of the claims of their body. Others pray most really as they walk. Still others like best to slip into a church on the way to work, or on the way home at night. God is our Father, and he does not tyrannize us with any stereotyped pattern. Prayer is discovered to be so much more than ' nudging the arm of the Almighty.' The proper spirit of approach is not ' do for me what I want ', but ' do with me what You want.' In the clear, lovely words of the Catechism of The United Church of Canada, ' Prayer is laying our lives open before God in gratitude and expectancy, casting ourselves on his mercy and love, telling him all the desires of our hearts, listening to his voice, and accepting his way for our lives.' Various parts of this whole go under the terms long used : invocation, thanksgiving, confession, petition, and intercession.

Throughout this little book I have purposely used a reverent ' you ', when addressing God, rather than the ancient ' thou '. I hope this will help to make these prayers more real. If it doesn't, go back to the old, familiar term.

Widespread gratitude for Dr. William Barclay's *The Plain Man's Book of Prayers* has led many women in many places to ask the publisher for a similar book to match their own lives. When I accepted the task of trying to write this I knew at sight, as did the publisher, that we couldn't call it ' a plain woman's book of prayers '; who wants to be a plain woman?

I have written prayers in present-day speech for morning and evening covering thirty-one days with a reading to accompany each one, Old Testament and New Testament alternating. Then I have added five extras for Sundays plus a reading and prayer for each of the main festival days. And to make the book yet more close to life I have added a number of brief prayers for personal occasions, and particular occupations. And for really good measure—living in the kind of world we do—a number of short graces.

This little book is meant to be only a stimulus—to help you to pray your own prayers in your own words. Don't wait for a crisis to arise—start now.

R. F. S.

PRAYERS
WITH BIBLE READINGS
FOR THIRTY-ONE DAYS

FIRST DAY

In the Morning

O God, I am glad to be alive. In this hour all nature stirs to meet the new day. But I would bring to you praise and adoration that only a human heart can bring.

I am fascinated by the mystery of darkness that surrenders to light;
I am fascinated by the fertility of earth, and the beauty of the skies;
I am fascinated by the many secrets long hidden, only now being discovered;
I am fascinated by the growing knowledge we have of human life and relationships.

I love the colour and shape and feel of things;
I love the sounds of nature, and the talk of my family and friends;
I love the prattle of little children, and the songs and laughter of young people;
I love so many hills and valleys I know, and seas, and rivers, and wild places;
I love the patterns of the fields, and their productiveness;
I love the way men and women have built homes to be together, helping and supporting each other.

Give me the courage, O God, in this quiet place to face the things I ought to face, before I go out to face my fellows.   AMEN

FIRST DAY

In the Evening

O God, I have learnt some things today, I never knew before;
I have met people today whom I have never met before;
I have thought about some things today I have never con-
sidered before.

But some things have been allowed to creep in, that now
I am sorry about :
Some things that I fully meant to do, I haven't done;
Some words I have spoken hastily, would have been better
unsaid;
Some relationships have been marred by my touchiness.

Forgive me for these things, and others, in which I have
failed you today, and fallen far below my best self; I
surrender this day to your mercy and keeping. Let me lie
down in peace, and after sound sleep, be ready to start
again tomorrow. AMEN

Daily Reading
PSALM 63 : 1–6

O God, thou art my God, I seek thee,
my soul thirsts for thee;
my flesh faints for thee,
as in a dry and weary land where no water is.
So I have looked upon thee in the sanctuary,
beholding thy power and glory.
Because thy steadfast love is better than life,
my lips will praise thee.
So I will bless thee as long as I live;
I will lift up my hands and call on thy name.

My soul is feasted as with marrow and fat,
and my mouth praises thee with joyful lips,
when I think of thee upon my bed,
and meditate on thee in the watches of the night.

SECOND DAY

In the Morning

O God, I don't want to take my good night's rest for granted:
Nor the safety and comfort of my home;
Nor the fresh feeling of health in my body;
Nor the renewed gifts of appreciation and thought;
Nor the love and loyalty of those closest to my life.

I want to begin this day with thankfulness, and continue
it with eagerness.
I shall be busy; let me set about things in the spirit of service
to you, and to my fellows, that Jesus knew in the carpenter's
shop in Nazareth.
I am glad that he drew no line between work sacred and
secular.

Take the skill that resides in my hands, and use it today;
Take the experience that life has given me, and use it;
Keep my eyes open, and my imagination alert, that I may
see how things look to others, especially the unwell, the
worried, the over-worked. For your love's sake.   AMEN

In the Evening

The day is done, O God, and I hush my heart again for
a few moments.
Forgive me, if I have wavered in my Christian witness when
I have been with others:
If I have hesitated at the crossroads of choice, when the
way needed courage;
If I have dreamed of great things, and failed in the little ones;

If I have gone about things solemnly, forgetting fun and
laughter;
If I have allowed myself to be so busy, that no one dare
tell me her troubles;
If I have shown impatience with anyone doing his best.

Bless this night, any I know, who do not pray for themselves :.
Any I know separated from those they love——and——
Any who still live together, whose hearts have drifted apart;
Any who have done things today, that now fill them with
shame;
Any who have suffered an accident, or in some other way,
found this a specially difficult day.
Be so real to us each that we may lie down in your peace.

AMEN

Daily Reading

JOHN I: 1–5, 11–14

In the beginning was the Word, and the Word was with God,
and the Word was God. He was in the beginning with God;
all things were made through him, and without him was not
anything made that was made. In him was life, and the life was
the light of men. The light shines in the darkness, and the
darkness has not overcome it. He came to his own home,
and his own people received him not. But to all who received
him, who believed in his name, he gave power to become
children of God; who were born, not of blood nor of the
will of the flesh nor of the will of man, but of God.

THIRD DAY

In the Morning

Eternal Father, let no remembrance of my faults of yesterday
hold me back from tackling life well today:
Save me from the burden of things that don't count;
Give me clear eyes to see things in proper perspective;
Grant me your spirit that I may renew my relationship
    With——who irritates me;
    With——who wears out my patience;
    With——who is so overbearing.

O God, it is easy to love the whole world, but hard to love
    the person one works next to;
O God, it is easy to campaign for world peace, but hard to
    contribute to the peace within my own home;
O God, it is easy to be fascinated with some new truth, and
    miss you in the thing I have known so long;
O God, it is easy to share my home, and possessions with
    people I like; teach me how to be generous toward others.

Enable me today to say something, or do something that
    will make a difference
    To the discouraged,
    To the inexperienced,
    To the despairing.

Let no selfish concern with my own affairs, shut me off from
any today. For your love's sake.   AMEN

In the Evening

O God, my Father, I worry sometimes at the day's end, when
    all is quiet:
I worry about those I love, especially——and——
    Help me to leave them in your love and care, while I do
    my very best for them,
    Help me to be sensible about them, and not give way to
    fussing.

I worry about my home sometimes; about——and——
  Save me from coveting the things of others, or the advertised goods I don't need,
  Save me from growing casual about the simple joys that once meant much to me.
I worry about my health sometimes; about——and——
  Enable me to be sensible in the expenditure of my energies;
  Enable me to take exercise and rest, enough to keep me fresh.
Bless especially this night all who lack the common decencies of life; all who hunger; all who belong nowhere.   AMEN

Daily Reading

PSALM 95 : 1–6

O come, let us sing to the Lord;
  let us make a joyful noise to the rock of our salvation!
Let us come into his presence with thanksgiving;
  let us make a joyful noise to him with songs of praise!
For the Lord is a great God,
  and a great King above all gods.
In his hand are the depths of the earth;
  the heights of the mountains are his also.
The sea is his, for he made it;
  for his hands formed the dry land.

O come, let us worship and bow down,
  let us kneel before the Lord, our Maker!

FOURTH DAY

In the Morning

O God, send me out into this day with eagerness, and bring me back to my rest with peace in my heart. Whatever the day holds, nothing can separate me from your love that surrounds me like the very air I breathe.

Let the door of my home, and of my heart, be open wide enough to receive gifts of friendship and joy this day, and narrow enough to shut out all pride, and self-sufficiency, and meanness.
Let me handle, as in your sight, all the practical things of this day;
Save me from wasting precious time dawdling.
Let no human obligation pass me by unawares,
  no needy one find me unsympathetic,
  no foolish one find me impatient,
  no good cause find me mean with my money.

I seek your special aid for those who must face hard tasks today:
  parents of difficult children;
  teachers of undisciplined scholars,
  social workers in dirty surroundings;
  counsellors who must try and save marriages;
  probation officers and magistrates and judges who must temper the law with mercy:
For your Kingdom's sake, O Lord.   AMEN

FOURTH DAY

In the Evening

Gracious God, I bring you my thanks for the experience of
this day:
So many good things have brought me joy, my home, with
its safety, its colours, its comfort, the meals served, and
the friendly talk shared, the flowers, both inside and out.
So many things have delighted my mind, books I have had
time to read, loaned, and owned, pictures that have shown
me a common thing in a new light.
So many things have quickened my spirit to love, those who
stand closest to my heart, little children who accept what
I can give, dumb creatures that need my care and protection.

Keep me ever mindful of those who make no response to
your love.   AMEN

Daily Reading

ROMANS 8: 35–39

Who shall separate us from the love of Christ? Shall tribulation, or distress, or persecution, or famine, or nakedness, or
peril, or sword? As it is written ' For thy sake we are being
killed all the day long; we are regarded as sheep to be
slaughtered.'
No, in all these things we are more than conquerors through
him who loved us. For I am sure that neither death, nor
life, nor angels, nor principalities, nor things present, nor
things to come, nor powers, nor height, nor depth, nor
anything else in all creation, will be able to separate us from
the love of God in Christ Jesus our Lord.

FIFTH DAY

In the Morning

I am thankful, O God, for every reminder of your holy love,
and your power, and your presence in this day to which I
waken :
Nothing can happen to me without your knowledge;
Nothing can involve me in joy, or sorrow without your care;
Nothing can tempt me beyond your power to keep me true;
Nothing in heaven or earth can destroy the peace you give
me which passes all understanding.

Let me not require of any other today a standard beyond
that which I require of myself;
Let me be as wide-eyed to others' good points as to my own;
Let me not ridicule anyone's stumbling efforts or take pleasure
in anyone's failure;
Let me be as ready to excuse another's mistakes as I am to
find excuses for my own;
Let me be as patient with others' lagging steps as you are
with mine;
Let me forgive others as freely and as really as I am myself
forgiven.

So teach me to live well this day. Through Christ my Lord.
AMEN

In the Evening

O God, I bring you thanks for the infinite variety of life :

For the trust of little children;
For the boundless curiosity of growing minds;
For the lovely grace and strength of young bodies;
For laughter and nonsense, and for serious intent;
For eagerness to adventure, and experiment;
For readiness to share, and to serve.

FIFTH DAY

Bless all the homes I know where there are young people;
Bless this night all whose work it is to direct their studies
    and share their sport;
Bless with good sense and high standards all in positions of
    leadership;
Bless with a lively awareness of responsibility, all who employ
    young people during their working hours, all who prepare
    interests for their minds and spirits, and entertainment
    for their bodies.
Bless with patience and a lively tolerance all older people
    who find it hard to understand youth.
In the name of Jesus of Nazareth, youth's true master.

AMEN

Daily Reading

PSALM 145: 9–16

The Lord is good to all,
    and his compassion is over all that he has made.

All thy works shall give thanks to thee, O Lord,
    and all thy saints shall bless thee!
They shall speak of the glory of thy kingdom,
    and tell of thy power,
to make known to the sons of men thy mighty deeds,
    and the glorious splendour of thy kingdom.
Thy kingdom is an everlasting kingdom,
    and thy dominion endures throughout all generations.

The Lord is faithful in all his words,
    and gracious in all his deeds.
The Lord upholds all who are falling,
    and raises up all who are bowed down.
The eyes of all look to thee,
    and thou givest them their food in due season.
Thou openest thy hand,
    thou satisfiest the desire of every living thing.

SIXTH DAY

In the Morning

O God, give your blessing this new day—
To all in my home; and
To those who are building new homes;
To those cherishing little children;
To those experienced in parenthood;
To those who enrich life's background—relations, play-mates, and friends.

O God, give your blessing this day—
To those in middle years
Those bearing burdens of education, industry, commerce, and science;
Those who preach and teach and guide people in community life;
Those who must keep standards high though nobody sees;
Those whose work brings small financial reward or encouragement.

O God, give your blessing today to—
Any whose work now outmatches their strength;
Any who can no longer expect advancement;
Any who find little satisfaction in what fills their day;
Any who because they are unfit, are tempted to give in;
Any who are nervy, impatient, and intolerant.

O God, give your blessing today to—
All in retirement and glad of it;
All bored by the loss of lifelong interests;
All troubled that they must not do what once they did;
All frail and all lonely ones in old age;
All coming by way of death to the brink of the new life.

Hold us all within your love today.   AMEN

SIXTH DAY

In the Evening

O God, You know how tired I am. Grant me rest of body
and mind; and strengthen my trust in your love.

Forgive me that some of my bright promises of this morning
have not been fulfilled.

Bring me gladly to another day, and its opportunities. To
your honour and glory.   AMEN

Daily Reading

MATTHEW 5: 1-12

Seeing the crowds, he went up on the mountain, and when
he sat down his disciples came to him. And he opened his
mouth and taught them, saying: 'Blessed are the poor in
spirit, for theirs is the kingdom of heaven. Blessed are those
who mourn for they shall be comforted. Blessed are the
meek, for they shall inherit the earth. Blessed are those who
hunger and thirst for righteousness, for they shall be satisfied.
Blessed are the merciful, for they shall obtain mercy. Blessed
are the pure in heart, for they shall see God. Blessed are the
peacemakers, for they shall be called sons of God. Blessed
are those who are persecuted for righteousness' sake, for theirs
is the kingdom of heaven. Blessed are you when men revile
you and persecute you and utter all kinds of evil against you
falsely on my account. Rejoice and be glad, for your reward
is great in heaven, for so men persecuted the prophets who
were before you.'

SEVENTH DAY

In the Morning

O God, the morning comes all too soon for those of us who
sleep well; let me not forget those who cannot sleep.
I am glad that as I go out I shall find myself today surrounded
By more loyal people than disloyal;
By more generous people than mean;
By more gracious people than rude;
By more happy people than the newspaper headlines might
lead me to think.

I bless you for
The countless happily-married people I know who never
get their names in print;
The countless unselfish people who never look first for
praise;
The countless courageous ones who might long ago have
given up but for you;
The countless people in unexpected places who translate
Christianity into daily living.

Give me the will to join them today. For Christ's sake.
AMEN

In the Evening

Gracious giver of all things good,
I bring you thanks for this day of life:
For gardens, and good roads,
For pleasant working conditions,
For companions and friends,
For cheerful colours, and laughter,
For books and papers,

For letters, for talk over the 'phone,
For pleasant clothes to put on, for appetising meals, and
for relaxation at the day's end.

I bring you my thanks now,
For any temptation this day resisted;
For any new thought that has pushed out my horizon;
For any new experience that has deepened my understand-
ing, for——
For every awareness of your holy love about me continually.

Grant me your gift of peace as sleep comes.   AMEN

Daily Reading

PSALM 121

I lift up my eyes to the hills.
From whence does my help come?
My help comes from the Lord,
  who made heaven and earth.

He will not let your foot be moved,
  he who keeps you will not slumber.
Behold, he who keeps Israel
  will neither slumber nor sleep.

The Lord is your keeper;
  the Lord is your shade
  on your right hand.
The sun shall not smite you by day,
  nor the moon by night.

The Lord will keep you from all evil;
  he will keep your life.
The Lord will keep
  your going out and your coming in
  from this time forth and for evermore

EIGHTH DAY

In the Morning

O God, open my inward eyes this day that I may see you at every turn; quicken my ears that I may hear you speak; and stir my whole being with gladness.

Deliver me from self-importance, and from pretence; make me mistress of my powers, that I may be servant to others. Let my acceptance of your forgiveness be so real that I may meet this day, unspoiled by anything, as I set about my routine tasks;
Keep me mindful of my blessings, that I may not look enviously on those of others;
Strengthen me when I suddenly meet
 Those who are better looking,
 Those who can be better dressed,
 Those who have more natural gifts,
 Those now more agile than I am,
 Those who are received for their charm wherever they go.

O God, enable me to keep today, the promises I have made in this quiet place before the day rushes on me.   AMEN

In the Evening

From early times, O God, others have turned aside at close of day to remember whose they are and whom they serve.
In simple homes and beside crude altars they have sought to pray as I do now: I pray
 For any for whom this has been a hard day;
 For any who have suddenly known fear;

For any suddenly covered with shame;
For any involved in an accident;
For any faced with a serious medical report;
For any in hospital for the first time;
For any so ill, that recovery is in doubt;
For any with a disease that baffles the specialists;
For any who have sinned against society, and are now
before the court.
Hold all such needy ones in your love, O Lord.   AMEN

Daily Reading

PSALM 51: 7–12

Purge me with hyssop, and I shall be clean;
  wash me, and I shall be whiter than snow.
Fill me with joy and gladness;
  let the bones which thou hast broken rejoice.
Hide thy face from my sins,
  and blot out all my iniquities.

Create in me a clean heart, O God,
  and put a new and right spirit within me.
Cast me not away from thy presence,
  and take not thy holy Spirit from me.
Restore to me the joy of thy salvation,
  and uphold me with a willing spirit.

NINTH DAY

In the Morning

My first thoughts, O God, are of wonder that you have
fashioned me for life here—and for fulfilment beyond this
earthly life that is mine.
Quicken the hearts of all dear to me, some of whom have
forgotten their divine destiny.

Let me live today in the reality of Christ's life here, his
death and triumphant resurrection that transforms everything
I know:
    Let me hold fast to his challenging words;
    Let me hold fast to his comforting words;
    Let me hold fast to his promised presence, now and till the
    end of the world.

Bless especially, this day, all who will come to the close of
life here; and
    All who are closest to them;
    All who minister to them, pastors, priests, doctors, nurses,
    friends;
    All at a distance, who receive their news with deep concern.

I rejoice that in your holy purpose life is all of a piece—
here and there.   AMEN

In the Evening

O God, I bless You for all those who have helped me on
my way today:
    Members of my family——and——
    My loyal friends——and——
    People I scarcely know——and——

Forgive me, if today, I have been only interested in my own
affairs, and unmindful of others.

Forgive me, if I have taken things too seriously, and forgotten fun and laughter.
Forgive me if I have allowed myself to be over-busy, with 'no time to stand and stare'.

I pray now, for any who have lacked joy this day:
  Any who have been without friendship;
  Any who have missed the common decencies;
  Any who have been without work;
  Any blind, deaf, or crippled;
  Any without strength of body;
  Any wanting the mind's clear light;
  Any without a sense of your presence;
  Any who look into the future without expectancy.
We are your children amidst the immensities of time, and eternity. Hold us in your keeping.   AMEN

Daily Reading

JOHN 14: 1–6

Let not your hearts be troubled; believe in God, believe also n me. In my Father's house are many rooms; if it were not o, would I have told you that I go to prepare a place for ou? And when I go and prepare a place for you, I will come gain and will take you to myself, that where I am you may e also. And you know the way where I am going.' Thomas aid to him, ' Lord, we do not know where you are going; how an we know the way?' Jesus said to him, ' I am the way, and he truth and the life; no one comes to the Father, but by me.'

TENTH DAY

In the Morning

It is wonderful, O God, to waken again refreshed, possessed of all my faculties.
It is wonderful to have people and things to get up for, and to serve all this day.

Let the sacredness of home life and human relationships outside come strongly through all I plan and do this day.
Let the wonder of human achievement be lightened by devotion to your good purposes in the world, here and afar.
Let those who devote their energies to peacemaking among the nations know your righteous strength and encouragement today.
Let those who till the soil and plant and harvest be good stewards of your earth entrusted to them, and make them ready to share with the needy.
Let those gifted above their fellows use their powers this day for the upbuilding of all things good and honest and true, and not for smashing-down.
Let all who labour to lighten the lot of others, especially—— and——among the many I know, have your blessing this day. For Jesus' sake.   AMEN

In the Evening

O God, I rejoice that you have lent me my body for life, my mind for thought, and have lighted within my spirit a flame that will never go out:
I have found life good today;
I have enjoyed the work I had to do;
I have enjoyed the friendship of those about me;
I have been glad to receive letters from many afar.

I pray that what has been good to me, may prove a worthy offering of love to you, as the night falls.

For everything undertaken in your strength, every problem solved, every human relationship strengthened, I bless you.
For every new task undertaken in your strength, every plan forwarded that I have been a little afraid of till now, I bless you.
For every stranger with whom I have talked, who promises to become a friend sharing common interests, I bless you.
For every secret temptation met in your strength and overcome; every cheery word spoken when it would have been easier to be stolidly unconcerned, I bless you.

Grant to all who have served with humility and courage, your gifts of deep satisfaction, and peace, as night falls over all.
AMEN

Daily Reading

MATTHEW 5: 13–16

' You are the salt of the earth; but if salt has lost its taste, how shall its saltness be restored? It is no longer good for anything except to be thrown out and trodden under foot by men.
' You are the light of the world. A city set on a hill cannot be hid. Nor do men light a lamp and put it under a bushel, but on a stand, and it gives light to all in the house. Let your light so shine before men, that they may see your good works and give glory to your Father who is in heaven.'

ELEVENTH DAY

In the Morning

I rejoice, O God, that you have wrought this world with exceeding beauty, that you have filled it with wonderful things. Let there be nothing in my thoughts or actions today that will mar that beauty, and that wonder.

The laws of nature and, no less, the longings of my own heart proclaim you :
    Let me seek out your will today and do it;
    Let me follow after your truth and love it;
    Let me trust you completely, whatever comes.

Deliver me today from prejudice and intolerance and sentimentality and hurtful talk.
Deliver me from laziness that contents itself with half truths, and from arrogance that thinks it knows all truth.
Deliver me from greed that seeks gain without labour, and from excitement in any form that cares not for its cost to others.

Enable me in your strength to persevere where I might too easily give up.
Enable me to replace shoddiness with beauty, evil with goodness.

Bless especially today all who will set down thoughts and opinions that others will read; all who will have part in the preparation and distribution of newspapers, magazines, and books; all who will introduce these into homes where there are little children, and receptive, unspoiled minds.   AMEN

In the Evening

For the colours of the sky at the day's end, O God, and for the quietness of night, I bring you my thanks :
    For birds homing through great spaces on confident wings;

For wild creatures that seek shelter out of sight of human
eyes;
For little children gathered in safely and early to sleep;
For all those weary and worn out who now enjoy the
simple joys of family life.

Bless especially this night, O God, all far from home——
and——and——and——all carrying on their work while
others sleep:
Those who have responsibility for planes, trains, ships,
and cars;
Those who minister to the sick, tend the mentally distressed,
restrain the reckless, or stand by those in sadness this night.

AMEN

Daily Reading

PSALM 92: 1–6

It is good to give thanks to the Lord,
to sing praises to thy name, O Most High;
to declare thy steadfast love in the morning,
and thy faithfulness by night,
to the music of the lute and the harp,
to the melody of the lyre.
For thou, O Lord, hast made me
glad by thy work;
at the works of thy hands I sing for joy.

How great are thy works, O Lord!
Thy thoughts are very deep!
The dull man cannot know,
the stupid cannot understand this.

TWELFTH DAY

In the Morning

Let your blessing today, O God, be with all those who cross
over my doorstep :
    All who go out to attend to their affairs,
    All who come in for any reason;
    Those going out to the bustle of the world,
    Those coming in to the warmth of the family circle.

I rejoice in the intimate joys of my home:
    In its safety and comfort and situation;
    In its security of good relationships;
    In its challenges shared and its strong supporting love.
I rejoice that personal values are here recognized :
    That the secret desires of any are the concern of all;
    That the successes of any are the pride of all;
    That the experiences of any are freely shared with all.
I rejoice in the many outside interests which centre in my
home:
    In friends and acquaintances who find here a good spirit;
    In music and books and good talk;
    In laughter and fun and family jokes.

I ask your blessing on all the homes dear to us : that of——
    and——and——and——
    On all new homes being established;——and——
    On all new parents, specially——and——
    On all growing grey together——and——
I ask your continued keeping of those dear to me in quiet
homes in country parts, in homes set down in busy cities,
in all places where your kingdom comes first in every
plan and your will is done gladly.   AMEN

TWELFTH DAY

In the Evening

Keep me courteous and cheerful, O God, at the day's end
when I am tired.
Help me to remember that others about me have been as busy.
Enable me to share something of beauty that I have seen
today.
Let our mealtime be a sharing of fellowship as well as
food and drink.
Where a thing of worth has been made or achieved make me
ready with praise.
And so strengthen in our daily relationships, things good and
glad. For your love's sake.   AMEN

Daily Reading

LUKE 10: 38–42

Now as they went on their way, he entered a village; and
a woman named Martha received him into her house. And
she had a sister called Mary, who sat at the Lord's feet
and listened to his teaching. But Martha was distracted
with much serving; and she went to him and said, 'Lord,
do you not care that my sister has left me to serve alone?
Tell her then to help me.' But the Lord answered her,
'Martha, Martha, you are anxious and troubled about many
things; one thing is needful. Mary has chosen the good
portion, which shall not be taken away from her.'

In the Morning

O God, I marvel that no two mornings are ever quite the same despite my routine:
That no single day is without its surprises;
That no least happening is beyond your knowledge;
That no ordinary task I have to do is outside your interest;
That no situation which poses a problem is beyond your solution;
That no distance is too far, though 'I take the wings of the morning';
That no isolation need spell loneliness, though 'I dwell in the uttermost parts of the sea';
That no sinful act of mine can put me outside your love and forgiveness and restoration.

Give me the courage I need today to face up to anybody, or anything I'm afraid of.
Give me conscientiousness about every part of the work entrusted to me.
Give me a spirit of cheer and friendliness. For your sake.
AMEN

In the Evening

In this quietness I would take time to look back over the day:
That Jesus has shown me what your very nature is has made all the difference to this day;
That Jesus has taught me to call you 'Father', has made all the difference to this day;
That Jesus has declared himself my Saviour and Lord triumphant, has made all the difference to this day;

That I have been called to witness to these great securities, has made all the difference to this day.

Forgive me for anything foolish I've been responsible for today.
Forgive me for anything I have allowed to worry me as though I did not know you.
Forgive me for any required task I have shirked, any decision I have evaded.
Forgive me if I have taken refuge in a lame excuse or a lie.
Forgive me if I have expected from others far more than I have been ready to give.
Forgive me if I have gossiped, or wasted my time, forgetting the high hopes with which I started the day.

In your presence, I own my faults——and——and I renew my vows. Grant me your peace now.　　　　AMEN

Daily Reading

PSALM 103: 8–13

The Lord is merciful and gracious, slow to anger and abounding in steadfast love. He will not always chide, nor will he keep his anger for ever. He does not deal with us according to our sins, nor requite us according to our iniquities. For as the heavens are high above the earth, so great is his steadfast love toward those who fear him; as far as the east is from the west, so far does he remove our transgressions from us. As a father pities his children, so the Lord pities those who fear him.

FOURTEENTH DAY

In the Morning

Eternal Father, I bring to you my first thoughts on waking,
so many lay claims upon me as the day advances.

Receive my thanks for safety through the night; for this
familiar setting.

Receive my thanks for my family and friends and their support.

Receive my thanks that each day I have my work to do and
strength to do it.

There are things about the earth and sky too great for me,
mountains and meteors and things that spell awe.

There are things so infinitesimal that they are beyond me,
atoms and electrons that I must take on trust.

There are things of such beauty and surprise that I am all
but moved to take the shoes from off my feet.

There are such countless ways in which the loving revelation
of the Bible is confirmed in everyday affairs.

For every good gift of yours which ministers to greater fullness
of life in this world, I bless you.   AMEN

In the Evening

As I bow in your presence, O God, my Father, let me be
more honest than I have been with others at times today.

Forgive me, if I have fallen to flattery today.
Forgive me, if I have set myself above others.
Forgive me, if I have stilled my conscience.
Forgive me, if I have lowered my standards.
Forgive me, if I have pretended things that are not so.
Forgive me, if I have criticised anyone unfairly.

Forgive me, if I have made it harder for anyone to live well today.

Forgive me, if I have been reluctant to follow your guidance in any matter.

For books and music, for letters and telephone-talk, I bring you my thanks, specially for——and——

For pictures, and films, and TV, I bring to you my thanks, specially for——and——

For crafts for my hands; and quiet, inspiring moments for my spirit, I bring you my thanks, especially for——and——

Hold in your loving care this night all whom I love, all whom I know, all whom I think of just now. AMEN

Daily Reading

LUKE 15: 3-7

So he told them this parable: 'What man of you, having a hundred sheep, if he has lost one of them, does not leave the ninety-nine in the wilderness, and go after the one which is lost, until he finds it? And when he has found it, he lays it on his shoulders, rejoicing. And when he comes home, he calls together his friends and his neighbours, saying to them, "Rejoice with me, for I have found my sheep which was lost." Even so, I tell you, there will be more joy in heaven over one sinner who repents than over ninety-nine righteous persons who need no repentance.'

FIFTEENTH DAY

In the Morning

As I open my eyes to the light, O God, let me open my heart
to all things good and true.

Let me not pass unseen any tiny new thing of grass or garden.

Let me not pass unseen any act of courage or of kindly
consideration.

Let me not overlook any way by which you are guiding me into
a deeper love.

Let me not overlook any way in which you are enriching my
understanding of life.

So quicken my faith in you and in your ways that this day
may be more meaningful:

That I may gladly put your will before my own;

That I may witness to you before those I meet;

That I may extend a helping hand to any in need.

Let me rejoice today with those who rejoice, and show
sympathy to those who suffer, are lonely, anxious, or bewildered. Let the simple things of my faith be utterly real.

AMEN

In the Evening

O Father, often I have blundered into your presence without
proper reverence; without a proper recollection of your loving
care; without proper words upon my lips; without a proper
readiness to listen.

In this quiet place, let me shed my haste;

In this quiet place, let me shed my pride;

In this quiet place, let me shed my self-sufficiency.

I am your child, a member of your world family as are those
I love, breathing and worshipping and thinking and serving
in your world.

I am the inheritor of all your loving promises, your revelation

through Jesus Christ, your purpose among men and women
to the end of the age.

I am a member of your Church in the world, a servant of your
will in politics, community, and family life; your witness
wherever people are found.

This night, hold in your love that means so much to me:
    The baffled, especially——and——
    The bored, especially——and——
    The bereaved, especially——and——
This night, hold in your love that means so much to me:
    The cynical, especially——and——
    The discouraged, especially——and——and all caught up
in situations of loss and misery.   AMEN

Daily Reading

PSALM 23: 1–6

The Lord is my shepherd, I shall not want;
  he makes me lie down in green pastures.
He leads me beside still waters;
  he restores my soul.
He leads me in paths of righteousness
  for his name's sake.

Even though I walk through the
  valley of the shadow of death,
I fear no evil; for thou art with me;
  thy rod and thy staff they comfort me.

Thou preparest a table before me
  in the presence of my enemies;
thou anointest my head with oil,
  my cup overflows.
Surely goodness and mercy shall follow me
  all the days of my life;
and I shall dwell in the house of the Lord
  for ever.

SIXTEENTH DAY

In the Morning

In sickness or health, in joy or grief, no day opens to find me alone:
I rejoice to realize you are always here;
I rejoice that you have given me human ties;
I rejoice in the many friends who are so loyal.

For duties that await me today, I ask your strength and skill. For things that puzzle me at this moment, I ask your patience. For tasks that have become tedious, I ask your gift of perseverance.

Let me remember all this day:
That people matter more than things;
That monetary reward matters less than honest service;
That faith and hope and love are the lasting things, and the greatest of these is love.

Bless any I love who are on holiday today; any who begin a new job; any who celebrate a birthday.

Let life be a better thing for somebody because we live in the world today. AMEN

In the Evening

O God, I bring you my thanks for what I have learned of human values from other women:
Those of the world's early days about whom I have read in Scripture and history;
Those of my forebears of whom I have been told or have seen photographs;

Those of my closer relations in my own lifetime, and experience.

I give thanks that all human souls are equally precious to you, and missed when they go astray:

Those who are headstrong and foolish;
Those who are simple and ignorant;
Those who are led into sin by others.

I give you thanks that skin colour counts for little; and that each has some special gift:

Those with physical graces:
Those with questing minds;
Those with spiritual perception above average.

Receive this day, O God, and hold safe, that which we each offer to you, through our own personalities: for Christ's sake.   AMEN

Daily Reading

LUKE 15:8–10

So he told them this parable: 'Or what woman, having ten silver coins, if she loses one coin, does not light a lamp and sweep the house and seek diligently until she finds it? And when she has found it, she calls together her friends and neighbours, saying, "Rejoice with me, for I have found the coin which I had lost." Even so, I tell you, there is joy before the angels of God over one sinner who repents.'

SEVENTEENTH DAY

In the Morning

O God, from you I come, and to you I go, and in your loving care I live and breathe and plan as this day begins.
I have a lot to do today:
   Give me the strength to do it well;
   Save me from being so busy that I forget life's true values;
   Keep me true to my best self, even when there is no one to see.

If results are disappointing, show me improvements that I can make.
If routine tasks drag, renew the interest I once had in them.
If I cannot see the outcome of the work I do today, give me patience.

Keep the edges of my mind clean, my thoughts pure.
Use my body to bring joy to others and to serve your purposes in the world.
Receive the worship of my loving spirit in all ways possible today.

I am not worthy of the least of your mercies, but without them this day could have no meaning.   AMEN

In the Evening

Grant me your peace and serenity, O Father, as I lie down to sleep.
And what blessings I ask for myself I ask for others in like need: for
   Any who lie down in humble homes;
   Any who lie down in fear;
   Any who are caught up in war;
   Any who are victims of others' carelessness;

Any who are involved in road accidents;
Any mystified by natural calamity;
Any in prisons and institutions of reform;
Any caught up in the toils of alcoholism;
Any subject to the domination of drug taking;
Any held captive within evil company;
Any who must face shame and begin again.

I am thinking especially of——and——known to you more than to any other and loved by you better than by any other. This is my faltering prayer, O God.   AMEN

Daily Reading

PSALM 139: 7–12

Whither shall I go from thy Spirit?
    Or whither shall I flee from thy presence?
If I ascend to heaven, thou art there!
    If I make my bed in Sheol, thou are there!
If I take the wings of the morning
    and dwell in the uttermost parts of the sea,
even there thy hand shall lead me,
    and thy right hand shall hold me.
If I say, 'Let only darkness cover me,
    and the light about me be night,'
even the darkness is not dark to thee,
    the night is bright as the day;
    for darkness is as light with thee.

EIGHTEENTH DAY

In the Morning

O God, enable me this very day to put my love into action:
To outreach with forgiveness to any I have hurt;
To show compassion to any who can use my strength;
To witness to the Christian faith as I know it.

Deliver me from all pretence.
Deliver me from all pettiness.
Deliver me from all foolish pride.

Let no opportunity surprise me, and pass, untaken.
Let no one live in loneliness that I can relieve.
Let no one find it hard to carry on, because of my criticism.

I bless you for countless fine men and women who serve you:
For all the good homes there are, good neighbours;
For devoted doctors and nurses and teachers;
For dedicated bishops, priests and pastors.

I ask your special blessing on
Those who have to do dangerous work today;
Those who have to make far-reaching decisions;
Those who bear the loneliness of the highest positions
of trust in our land.

Let me live worthy of a place in such glorious company.

AMEN

In the Evening

O God, in this age of so many gadgets and new tools, it
is easy to forget that men and women matter most.

In this age of great scientific and technological advance, it
is hard to hold to true values;

EIGHTEENTH DAY

In this age of rapid transport, running hither and thither, it
is easy to miss you near at hand;
In this age of many nations coming newly to birth it is easy
to feel national superiority;
In this bewildering age of outer-space it is easy to under-
value inner peace.

For every experience of your holiness, your justice, your
mercy, I bless you.
For every preacher and teacher and author who has helped
me to such, I bless you.
For every friend, every acquaintance, every stranger who has
deepened my awareness of you, I give thanks.

So let this day end, as it began, with love and praise.

AMEN

Daily Reading

LUKE 15: 11–16

And he said, 'There was a man who had two sons; and
the younger of them said to his father, "Father, give me the
share of property that falls to me." And he divided his
living between them. Not many days later, the younger
son gathered all he had and took his journey into a far country,
and there he squandered his property in loose living. And
when he had spent everything, a great famine arose in that
country, and he began to be in want. So he went and joined
himself to one of the citizens of that country, who sent him
into his fields to feed the swine. And he would gladly have
fed on the pods that the swine ate; and no one gave him
anything.'

NINETEENTH DAY

In the Morning

O God, I praise you with my earliest breath for what I enjoy
so much:
    For the freshness of the morning calling to new ventures;
    For the hard work of the middle hours of the day calling
    for perseverance;
    For the promise of rest and relaxation at the day's end.

I praise you that these good things are not mine alone, but
shared with family and friends and fellow workers:
    I cannot fully know today their secret joys;
    I cannot fully know their hidden needs;
    I cannot fully know their treasured plans.

Use me, this day, in some humble way, to minister to those
who seek your help as they pray themselves:
    Where there is a wound that hurts, let me bring a new
    sensitivity;
    Where there is domination, let me bring a gentle gift of
    respect;
    Where there is friction, let me pour the cool balm of
    understanding;
    Where there is insecurity, let me breathe sweet confidence.

So in your keeping, bless our going out and our coming in.
AMEN

In the Evening

Almighty God, I marvel that you have entrusted to me
    A heart to love,
    A mind to think and explore,
    A will to follow your lead through life.

I marvel that you have made me part of your large and

wonderful purpose: forgive me where I have forgotten this in any situation or faltered in my loyalty.

I cannot deserve your loving care; I have sinned so often and have not always been so sorry about it as I ought to have been.

I bless you for many ordinary, honest people who have served me today—some of them within the Church, some without.

I ask your blessing on those who through farms tended, and children taught, have helped you to meet the needs of bodies and minds today.

I seek your compassion on all who are lonely at nightfall, far from those they love, or in any other way lacking human help. For your love's sake.   AMEN

Daily Reading
ISAIAH I: 16–18

Wash yourselves; make yourselves clean;
remove the evil of your doings from before my eyes;
cease to do evil, learn to do good;
seek justice, correct oppression;
defend the fatherless, plead for the widow.

Come now, let us reason together, says the Lord:
though your sins are like scarlet,
they shall be as white as snow;
though they are red like crimson,
they shall become like wool.

TWENTIETH DAY

In the Morning

O God, it is wonderful to waken again sure of your love:
  To know that nothing can happen today without your
  knowledge;
  To know that no foolishness of mine can frustrate you
  as it does me;
  To know that no deliberate sin of mine can cut me off
  from your care;
  To know that nothing is too bad for your forgiveness.

It is wonderful to know myself part of your world family,
  So human, and so strangely diverse,
  So richly gifted with skills,
  So needy and so much alike at heart.
It is wonderful to recall that your only begotten son, our
  Saviour, was born of a Hebrew mother; rejoiced in the
  faith of a Syrophoenician woman; made himself available
  to questioning Greeks who came saying, 'We would see
  Jesus'; trod the sorrowful way, his Cross carried by a
  Cyrenian with a black skin; received at death the tribute
  of a Roman soldier, 'Certainly, this was a righteous man!'
It is wonderful that in his kingdom, there is neither
  Greek nor Jew, racial discrimination;
  Barbarian nor Scythian, cultural discrimination;
  Bond nor free, social discrimination;
  Male nor female, sex discrimination,
But that all are one, and precious. For this assurance I
bless you. Let me remember it today, as I meet people.
                                                        AMEN

TWENTIETH DAY

In the Evening

Let every part of this day's labour and leisure occupations
that cannot bear your sight be cast away.

Forgive me if I have allowed pride to dictate any action:
If I have been lacking in love;
If I have shown intolerance;
If I have wasted precious hours;
If I have spoken hasty words;
If I have gossiped of another;
If I have for a moment lost the individual in the crowd;
If I have forgotten that I hold in trust to you this swift
and lovely gift of life.

Grant me your peace now, which passeth all understanding,
and the sweet gift of sleep.   AMEN

Daily Reading

LUKE 15: 17–21

But when he came to himself he said, 'How many of my
father's hired servants have bread enough and to spare, but I
perish here with hunger! I will arise and go to my father,
and I will say to him, " Father, I have sinned against heaven
and before you; I am no longer worthy to be called your son;
treat me as one of your hired servants." ' And he arose and
came to his father. But while he was yet at a distance, his
father saw him and had compassion, and ran and embraced
him and kissed him. And the son said to him, ' Father, I have
sinned against heaven and before you; I am no longer worthy
to be called your son.'

TWENTY-FIRST DAY

In the Morning

O Lord, enable me to keep my vision clear, my step light,
and my heart loyal, as I go out today.

Let your holy will be my passion:
  Nothing more,
  Nothing less,
  Nothing else.

Grant to us all, a vision of this land free from
  The servitude of material things;
  The ugliness of national pride;
  The smugness of blind success;
  The sin of political insincerity;
  The ugliness and dullness and waste of evil.

With our warehouses full and our tables well-spread, save
us from
  Lack of knowledge of the rest of the world;
  Unconcern for others' desperate needs;
  Unreadiness to share our good things, even at great cost.

And all day and into the night, let us bear each others'
  burdens:
So bind us together more closely as your world family.

AMEN

In the Evening

O God, my Father, I am tired. This has been a long day.
As your stars shine steadily in the immensities of space,
and your gentle night winds cool the heated weary earth,
so let your peace and renewal come to my spirit.

I bring you my deep thanks for those of your children who
have served the common good this day:
In shop, and office, and market place;
In hospital, in college, in court of law;
In board room, committee room, lecture room;
In the meeting place of Parliament;
In the council halls of the United Nations;
In the farmhouse and barn, and on the soil where the
seasons move endlessly.

Gather us in now, as night covers us, and grant us renewal
of strength and purpose for when the new day comes.

AMEN

Daily Reading

PSALM 34: 1–4, 8, 13–15

I will bless the Lord at all times;
  his praise shall continually be in my mouth.
My soul makes its boast in the Lord;
  let the afflicted hear and be glad.
O magnify the Lord with me,
  and let us exalt his name together!
I sought the Lord, and he answered me,
  and delivered me from all my fears.

O taste and see that the Lord is good!
  Happy is the man who takes refuge in him!

Keep your tongue from evil,
  and your lips from speaking deceit.
Depart from evil and do good;
  seek peace, and pursue it.
The eyes of the Lord are toward the righteous,
  and his ears toward their cry.

TWENTY-SECOND DAY

In the Morning

As the new day comes, and I waken from sleep, I remember
all those who have been on duty through the hours of
darkness:
Nurses and doctors and anxious relations;
Pilots of planes and their crews;
Captains of ships, and those who sail with them;
Engine drivers and their mates;
Night editors and their staff;
Caretakers of public buildings;
Firemen and police officers;
Prison warders and taxi men;
Milkmen and newspaper boys;
Radio operators and rescue teams.
I remember those cheated of sleep by worry, by homelessness,
by revelry; those who have used the dark hours in which
to plan evil—safe breakers, and burglars and thieves; and
alcoholics, drug pedlars, and rogues.
I hardly know anything of the world of some of these and
cannot pray intelligently, but they are human beings, and
they have their deep needs too. Strengthen in service today
all who minister to the outcast in your name, remembering
Christ's care for all such.   AMEN

TWENTY-SECOND DAY

In the Evening

Father, this has been a day full of interest; and I bring you thanks for it:
If I have spoiled any of its splendours by carrying forward grudges I should have forgotten;
If I have marred any of its opportunities by unconcern for others;
If I have withheld clean laughter that might have lightened another's load;
Forgive me, O God.

I bless you for my dear ones, who know all about me, and still love me——and——and——
I bless you for my close friends, who are aware of my weaknesses, but are still so loyal——and——and——   AMEN

Daily Reading

LUKE 15: 22–27

But the father said to his servants, 'Bring quickly the best robe, and put it on him; and put a ring on his hand, and shoes on his feet; and bring the fatted calf and kill it, and let us eat and make merry; for this my son was dead, and is alive again; he was lost and is found.' And they began to make merry.

Now his elder son was in the field; and as he came and drew near to the house, he heard music and dancing. And he called one of the servants and asked what this meant. And he said to him, 'Your brother has come, and your father has killed the fatted calf, because he has received him safe and sound.'

In the Morning

This new day is your good gift to me; let me accept it with
   eagerness and use it well.
Grant that every word I speak may be fit for you to hear;
   That every plan I make, may be fit for you to bless;
   That every deed I do, may be fit for you to share.

Keep me courageous if things should prove exacting;
Keep me cheerful if things should prove dull;
Keep me unruffled if the unexpected should occur;
Keep me patient should I be involved with the foolish actions
   of others.

So may I find my way hopefully through this day, spending
   my love for your sake, my energies and my time.   AMEN

In the Evening

In the quietness which is your gift at the day's end, O Father,
   draw near to all who have special need of you this night:
   All crushed in spirit;
   All estranged from those they love;
   All who lack any thread of purpose in life.

Draw as near to those who can hardly contain their joy, or
   help but share their good news, and tell their secret plans:
   All newly fallen in love;
   All this day married;
   All who have just become parents;

All who have entered a new house;
All whose work plans have prospered;
All who have just passed their exams;
All who have at last received a telegram bearing good news
after long waiting;
All who have entered into some new spiritual experience,
that has changed the world for them.

Let your rich blessing be mine this night, and bless all
whom I love, in the quiet countryside and in the crowded
city. I think of——   AMEN

Daily Reading

PSALM 118: 19–24

Open to me the gates of righteousness,
   that I may enter through them
   and give thanks to the Lord.

This is the gate of the Lord;
   the righteous shall enter through it.

I thank thee that thou hast answered me
   and hast become my salvation.
The stone which the builders rejected
   has become the chief cornerstone.
This is the Lord's doing;
   it is marvellous in our eyes.
This is the day which the Lord has made;
   let us rejoice and be glad in it.

TWENTY-FOURTH DAY

In the Morning

O God, I have no way of telling at the day's beginning,
Who will come to my door on an errand of business or
friendship;
Who will arrive to be my guest in my home or to sit at
my table.

Let me show loving care this day in the cleaning of my
house, the buying of my stores, the cooking of my meals.
Let me show loving care this day in the tending of my linen,
the tidying of my cupboards, the doing of my flowers.
Let me show loving care in the freshness of my person and
the neatness and niceness of my clothes.

From the beginning of homemaking in modest tents on
the sand, women have served their families, and their guests.
From the beginning of homemaking in simple homes of
baked mud, women have whitewashed and scrubbed, and
set out their pretty things.
From the beginning of more comfortable houses, with hand-
woven carpets and furniture of cunning craftsmanship,
women have kept open house.

May Christ be my guest this day.   AMEN

In the Evening

O God, if the happiness of my situation has deceived me
into a false reliance on myself today, I am sorry.

O God, if any member of my family or any guest beneath
my roof has lacked what you counted on me to give, I
am sorry.

O God, if I have allowed pride of possessions or in good

management to lead me to fussing over the less important things, I am sorry.

Accept, for the sake of Christ my Lord, what I have tried to do through and in my home.

Accept, for the sake of Christ my Lord, what I have cooked, and set upon my table.

Accept for the sake of Christ my Lord, my sweet, clean beds, my flowers, and books.

Accept, for the sake of Christ my Lord, my fire kindled on the hearth, and the chairs pulled round for talk.   AMEN

Daily Reading

JOHN 12: 1–7

Six days before the Passover, Jesus came to Bethany, where Lazarus was, whom Jesus had raised from the dead. There they made him a supper; Martha served, and Lazarus was one of those at table with him. Mary took a pound of costly ointment of pure nard and anointed the feet of Jesus and wiped his feet with her hair; and the house was filled with the fragrance of the ointment. But Judas Iscariot, one of his disciples (he who was to betray him), said, 'Why was this ointment not sold for three hundred denarii and given to the poor?' This he said, not that he cared for the poor but because he was a thief, and as he had the money box he used to take what was put into it. Jesus said, 'Let her alone, let her keep it for the day of my burial.'

In the Morning

Once again, O God, the dawn ushers in the busy, demanding hours of day: early and late, keep me true to my promises to you in this quiet place.

Hold me:
  In any moment of temptation;
  In any test of ordinary routine;
  In any moment when others praise;
  In any experience of delight;
  In any hour when doubt appears;
  In any unexpected demand.

With all the enticing rewards of earth in sight, let me choose your way today.
With the joyous consent of all my faculties, let me serve you as I can.

So keep me through this day, and at nightfall bring me to my rest in peace.   AMEN

In the Evening

O God, I marvel that Jesus came right into the life about him on earth, walking with sandalled feet the dusty roads, Choosing his friends;
  Rising early to refresh his spirit in prayer;
  Patiently teaching and preaching to crowds;
  Interrupting his plans to restore a son to his sorrowing mother, a widow;

Associating with people of no social standing;
Making time for the simplicities of children;
Showing mercy and compassion to the sick;
Washing the feet of quarrelsome disciples.

Let his wonderful spirit lay hold of me more and more as I got out each day to serve, and come in each night to rest, for his dear sake.

Forgive me, if today I have failed in any task because I have been prideful.
Forgive me, if I failed because I have been over-ambitious.
Forgive me, if I have failed because I did not ask your help.

Bless this night all my dear ones whose faces come before me in this quietness——and——
Bless this night all with whom I have had any dealings this day——and——and—— AMEN

Daily Reading

JOHN 13: 1–4

Now before the feast of the Passover, when Jesus knew that his hour had come to depart out of this world to the Father, having loved his own who were in the world, he loved them to the end. And during supper, when the devil had already put it into the heart of Judas Iscariot, Simon's son, to betray him, Jesus, knowing that the Father had given all things into his hands, and that he had come from God and was going to God, rose from supper, laid aside his garments, and girded himself with a towel.

In the Morning

O God, it is increasingly easy for me to see what life ought
to be, given a new day, but—
 I do not often live through a day as I would like to;
 I do not often sustain an attitude of love in all things;
 I do not often trust myself to your sustaining power as I
 should;
 I do not often forgive, as I am myself forgiven by you.

This is a new day.
 Let it be a good day in every way. May I be more loving,
 more courteous, more cheerful.

Bless especially all those who tend the sick and the frail
and aged;
Bless especially all who waken to responsibilities they feel
too great for them;
Bless especially all who seek a real faith and experience of
your keeping, redeeming love.
Bless especially——and——and——for whom this day might
well have lasting significance.   AMEN

In the Evening

O Father, your nearness can transform the lowliest task and
the loneliest hour.
Forgive me, if today I have failed to choose your way and
to do your will.
Forgive me, if I have behaved very much like everybody
else where things were a little awkward.
Forgive me, if I have been too rushed to show concern for
the needs of others.

Forgive me, if anything else I have failed in in this day
embarrasses me now, and brings excuses to my lips.

You have filled this earthly life I share with wonderful oppor-
tunities to know:
  The satisfaction of good workmanship;
  The delights of family life;
  The clean joys of physical fitness;
  The challenge of new ideas;
  The happiness of good company;
  The beauty of music and song;
  The inwardness of spiritual reality.

Let me not hold back for fear of the cost of your way of life
or for want of trust in your love and care. Now or ever.
                                                      AMEN

Daily Reading

PSALM 116: 1–8

I love the Lord, because he has heard
    my voice and my supplications.
Because he inclined his ear to me,
    therefore I will call on him as long as I live.
The snares of death encompassed me;
    the pangs of Sheol laid hold on me;
I suffered distress and anguish.
Then I called on the name of the Lord:
    'O Lord, I beseech thee, save my life!'

Gracious is the Lord, and righteous;
    our God is merciful.
The Lord preserves the simple;
    when I was brought low, he saved me.
Return, O my soul, to your rest;
    for the Lord has dealt bountifully with you.

For thou hast delivered my soul from death,
    my eyes from tears, my feet from stumbling.

In the Morning

Eternal God, it is wonderful to keep on finding out things.
The best I have to hold to my heart are those shown me in
the life and words of Jesus Christ:

I thank you for his coming into history in a little country
on this earth, to walk its crowded roads, and city streets
and to mingle with men and women;

I thank you for the fulfilling of your long-promised revelation
in him, in his life and message, his death, and rising again;

I thank you for those who saw in his steady eyes dividing
the false from the true, in his steady step going courageously
upon his way, your very nature;

I thank you for those scribes among them who set down, in
the words that have become the New Testament, the discoveries and challenges of his kingdom for me.

I bless you for all who have preserved and translated and
printed this record of life's most precious allegiance. To
your honour and glory.   AMEN

In the Evening

Gracious God, I find I have been so preoccupied with my
own concerns today.

I have spared very little thought since this morning for
things eternal.

I have been slow to see your purpose being worked out in
the world all about me:

The sun has risen in hope,

And shone in life-giving power,

And set in colourful glory;

The stars have come out,

With the gentle moon riding high,

And the cool darkness bringing rest.

Bless, as I remember them before you now——and——and all whom I love.

Bless, as I remember them before you now——and——and all in special need.

Bless, as I remember them before you now, those with great responsibilities, in this land——and——

Bless, as I remember them before you now, the Secretary of the United Nations——and all others devoted to real peace-making.

Bless, as I remember them before you now——and all at any world conference table. To your glory.   AMEN

Daily Reading

JOHN 14: 15–17, 25–27

'If you love me, you will keep my commandments. And I will pray the Father, and he will give you another Counsellor, to be with you for ever, even the Spirit of truth, whom the world cannot receive, because it neither sees him nor knows him; you know him, for he dwells with you, and will be in you. These things I have spoken to you, while I am still with you. But the Counsellor, the Holy Spirit, whom the Father will send in my name, he will teach you all things, and bring to your remembrance all that I have said to you. Peace I leave with you; my peace I give to you; not as the world gives do I give to you. Let not your hearts be troubled, neither let them be afraid.'

In the Morning

In simple words, O Lord, I bring you thanks for your life
which stirs within me:
For the freshness and beauty of this morning;
For the day's long hours stretching before me, for work
and play.

Let me not leave unrepaired any of yesterday's wrongs or
break any of this moment's promises:
Keep me from the sins of showiness and shoddiness;
Keep me from any temptation to lower my standards.
Let me not rise from this moment's worship and praise and
rush ahead unmindful of its reality:
Keep me faithful and diligent this day;
Keep me chaste in thought, and honourable.
Let me be responsive to your guidance, and thankful for it,
in any crossroad of choice:
Speak to me through remembrance of Scripture;
Speak to me through circumstances and friends.

And these blessings I ask for myself, I ask for all those
near and dear to me. AMEN

In the Evening

The hours of this day have flown. For all the good things
you have given me, I give thanks, O God.

Bless in this evening hour, any
Who have known joy in the gift of a little child;
Who have made a new friend or met an old one.
Bless in this evening hour, any
Who have suffered accident, or known fear;
Who have received a serious diagnosis.

Bless in this evening hour, any
  Who have been far from home and lonely;
  Who have behaved shamefully and regret it.
Bless in this evening hour, any
  Who have found new courage and strength;
  Who have made good decisions and are glad.

Quicken the hearts and minds of men and women in positions
of leadership everywhere to choose the costly way of peace
and understanding, and trust.

Banish from your lovely world those things which we have
introduced to its spoiling.

Give patience and generous hearts and clear minds to all
who serve your will, that the time may come when it may
be done on earth as in heaven.   AMEN

Daily Reading

MALACHI 3: 16–18

Then those who feared the Lord spoke with one another;
the Lord heeded and heard them, and a book of remembrance
was written before him of those who feared the Lord and
thought on his name. 'They shall be mine, says the Lord of
hosts, my special possession on the day when I act, and I
will spare them as a man spares his son who serves him.
Then once more you shall distinguish between the righteous
and the wicked, between one who serves God and one who
does not serve him.'

In the Morning

O God, I am glad that with the dawn, comes once more the
call of Christ:
Help me to respond with the whole of my personality as
did those by Galilee;
Help me to count no cost of position or possessions too
much to surrender;
Help me to enter joyously into his fellowship, along with
others who share it;
Help me to lend to his Church in the world the energies
and gifts of money and mind he has entrusted to me as his
good steward.

Let no action or word of mine this day prove a stumbling
block to any other.
Let no action or word of mine this day be unworthy of my
Lord and Master, Jesus Christ.
And what help and guidance to this end I seek for myself,
I ask for others too, especially for——and——and——

AMEN

In the Evening

O God, from everlasting to everlasting, I bless you for this
day and for my awareness of your care throughout all its
hours.
Sometimes, I have been too busy to think of this consciously;
Sometimes, I have just had to go ahead in trust;
Sometimes, new situations have sprung on me of a sudden.
But you have not failed me in any of your promises, in any
sudden need I have known, in any moment of indecision:
You have surrounded me with neighbours, and companions;

You have strengthened me through friends, and members of my family.

I ask your blessing now, at nightfall, on all who have lived generously and cheerfully today, and have done a good day's work.

I ask your blessing now on all who have met difficulties unguessed by most and have kept on;

I ask your blessing now on any who have blundered, but have found courage to try again.

None of us can live well without your blessing nor lie down in peace. We know this. AMEN

Daily Reading

ROMANS 12: 2, 9–13

Do not be conformed to this world but be transformed by the renewal of your mind, that you may prove what is the will of God, what is good and acceptable and perfect. Let love be genuine; hate what is evil, hold fast to what is good; love one another with brotherly affection; outdo one another in showing honour. Never flag in zeal, be aglow with the Spirit, serve the Lord. Rejoice in your hope, be patient in tribulation, be constant in prayer. Contribute to the needs of the saints, practise hospitality.

In the Morning

O God, it seems no time since I put out the light and now the
new day has come:
  I rejoice in the renewal of sleep;
  I rejoice in another chance to think and feel;
  I rejoice in another chance to love and serve.

While I enjoy my home and family, let me not be unmindful
of many needy ones in your world family:
  All who lack knowledge of your Gospel;
  All who lack clothing and food and shelter;
  All who lack work to do, and a hope to fasten on.

I pray especially for all who face this day without health
and strength of body or mind:
  All who start it without interest;
  All who face the earning of money with anxiety;
  All hindered, and hurt by alcoholism, and any other secret
  addiction.

Guide and encourage in your own good way, all who approach
new responsibilities this day, shy, or unsure:
  All who receive little new lives into their care;
  All who sit examinations, having done their best;
  All setting out on long journeys, nervous of their reception.

Whatever our special needs, your wisdom and love and
care are sufficient. Whatever we are called to go through,
nothing can utterly overwhelm us. In this security of spirit,
is our strength, now and always.   AMEN

In the Evening

O God, my Father, you know all that has made up today:
Its joys and perplexities;
Its promises broken;
Its opportunities not seized.
O God, forgive me for my share in these things today:
For my slowness to respond;
For my dullness of mind;
For my eyes lifted afar when beauty was all about me.
O God, strengthen me with a greater dependence:
Only in your way of life is satisfaction;
You have made me for yourself;
You have set me in this wonderful world to love and
serve.
O God, bless my coming-in this night as you blessed my
going-out at the day's beginning.   AMEN

Daily Reading

PSALM 19: 7–11

The law of the Lord is perfect, reviving the soul;
   the testimony of the Lord is sure, making wise the simple;
the precepts of the Lord are right, rejoicing the heart;
   the commandment of the Lord is pure, enlightening the eyes;
the fear of the Lord is clean, enduring for ever;
   the ordinances of the Lord are true, and righteous altogether.
More to be desired are they than gold, even much fine gold;
   sweeter also than honey and drippings of the honeycomb.

Moreover by them is thy servant warned;
   in keeping them there is great reward.

In the Morning

In your fatherly wisdom, O God, you have given me the
night for sleep, and the day for service:
Let this day be marked by joyous service;
Let me worship you and honour your will;
Let me think of others' needs as well as of my own.

Make me mindful that all these good gifts so richly given
are yours also to curtail:
I would not take my health and strength for granted;
I would not take my home comforts for granted;
I would not use my talents except as your steward.

Make me generous with my money as well as with my time,
sponsoring aid to others:
I would not handle my pay packet lightly;
I would not forget the ministry of the Church;
I would not overlook the hungry and the ill-clad I never
meet.

Let me live today, as a member of my intimate circle and
as a member of my community, my country, and your great
world family. For Christ's sake.   AMEN

In the Evening

O God, no tongue can fashion praise worthy of all your
loving care;
O God, no tongue can formulate a list of all your loving gifts.
Accept my poor blundering efforts, my deeds of love where
words fail;
Accept my joy in good books, as an offering of praise
to you for all truth;
Accept my delight in music, as an offering of praise for
all uplifting experiences.

Through the words of the Old and New Testaments I have
   come to know you:
   Through the gentleness and love of early Sunday-school
   teachers, faithful and dear;
   Through the storytellers who have clothed the great deeds
   of other days with vividness;
   Through preachers, and discussion leaders, who have translated for me the spirit of Christ.

O Lord, let me not fail in doing for others, what these have
   done for me:
   Enliven the thoughts that enter my mind;
   Quicken the readiness of my hands to serve;
   Receive the utter devotion of my spirit.   AMEN

Daily Reading

GALATIANS 5: 22–26

But the fruit of the Spirit is love, joy, peace, kindness,
goodness, faithfulness, gentleness, self-control; against such
there is no law. And those who belong to Christ Jesus have
crucified the flesh with its passions and desires.

If we live by the Spirit, let us also walk by the Spirit.
Let us have no self-conceit, no provoking of one another,
no envy of one another.

PRAYERS WITH
BIBLE READINGS
FOR FIVE SUNDAYS

FIRST SUNDAY

Reading

LUKE 4: 16-19

And he came to Nazareth, where he had been brought up; and he went to the synagogue, as his custom was, on the sabbath day. And he stood up to read; and there was given him the book of the prophet Isaiah. He opened the book and found the place where it was written, 'The Spirit of the Lord is upon me, because he has anointed me to preach good news to the poor. He has sent me to proclaim release to the captives and recovering of sight to the blind, to set at liberty those who are oppressed, to proclaim the acceptable year of the Lord.'

In the Morning

O God, I am tempted to stay in bed this morning; but to
do that I must miss church:
The privilege of worship;
The fellowship of those I know there;
The opportunity for community witness.
And all the remainder of the day, I shall be in a scramble
to do what I have to do:
To see to the meals;
To tidy up the house;
To write the letters and pay the visits I should.
Bless this day all who prepare to lead in worship:
Quicken their minds;
Order their words clearly;
And give them joy in proclaiming the Gospel.
Bless all who assemble for worship:
In great cathedrals and churches;
In tiny chapels and hospital wards;
Upon ships at sea and over the wireless.

Draw especially near to those sad at heart, needing comfort:
   Perplexed and uncertain, needing guidance;
   Ashamed, needing forgiveness;
   Strong and eager, echoing back the joy of those who worshipped on the first day of the risen Christ.
Bless especially just now all newly come into discipleship:
   In my own land——and——
   In lands where there is persecution;
   In places of isolation, where few share regular worship, and witness.
Let this day be to each of us, a rich experience. For your love's sake.   AMEN

In the Evening

As night closes round me, O God, I bless you for what this day has brought me from you
   Through the words of the prophets,
   Through the poems of the psalmists,
   Through the history of the past.
I bless you for what has come to me afresh
   Through the Gospels and Epistles,
   Through the prayers and hymns;
   Through the preaching from the pulpit.
I bless you for the fellowship of the congregation, especially for——
   Let us be outward reaching in our witness;
   Let us be understanding and tolerant;
   Let us be unwearying in our service.   AMEN

SECOND SUNDAY

Reading

MARK 2: 23–28

One sabbath he was going through the grainfields; and as they made their way his disciples began to pluck ears of grain. And the Pharisees said to him, 'Look, why are they doing what is not lawful on the sabbath?' And he said to them, 'Have you never heard what David did, when he was in need and was hungry, he and those who were with him: how he entered the house of God, when Abiathar was high priest, and ate the bread of the Presence, which it is not lawful for any but the priests to eat, and also gave it to those who were with him?' And he said to them, 'The sabbath was made for man, not man for the sabbath; so the Son of man is lord even of the sabbath.'

In the Morning

O God, I thank you for this day of rest and worship.
I need it, because I cannot crowd my life in to the space and speed of working hours;
I need the silence that of all seven days this day brings;
I need time in which to recall whose I am and why I am here;
I need the unhurried love of those about me, shining in friendly eyes;
I need the unhurried sharing of thoughts, experiences, dreams;
I need beautiful books, and music, and song, so easily pushed aside in the busy week;
I need time to remember in prayer before you, my family and friends; missionaries and volunteer workers who speak your message in other lands in strange languages difficult to master and in trying unhealthy climates.

I need time to remember in prayer before you, all young men and women faintly hearing the challenge to this kind of service. Hush their hearts to hear and quicken their wills to offer for your kingdom on earth the best they have.

I need time to remember in prayer before you, all preachers and teachers, and principals of colleges and their staffs, devoting their lives to scholarship and the training of others who will interpret your growing revelation to men and women.

I need time to remember especially——and——

Whatever our task in your world, enable us to do it, and keep us faithful. For Christ's sake. Strengthen us in the daily knowledge that his hand is upon the whole of our lives—the whole. AMEN

In the Evening

O God, as I surrender myself to sleep to rise ready for the ordinary weekday activities tomorrow, let me be refreshed.

As I meet with others tomorrow with whom I do not share life on Sunday, strengthen and enrich our relationships.

Give me joy and eagerness and courage where I must quickly decide my line of action amid conflicting values.

And keep me humble and natural in all I do for you.

AMEN

THIRD SUNDAY

Reading

MATTHEW 28: 1–8

Now after the sabbath, toward the dawn of the first day of the week, Mary Magdalene and the other Mary went to see the sepulchre. And behold, there was a great earthquake; for an angel of the Lord descended from heaven and came and rolled back the stone, and sat upon it. His appearance was like lightning, and his raiment white as snow. And for fear of him the guards trembled and became like dead men. But the angel said to the women, 'Do not be afraid; for I know that you seek Jesus who was crucified. He is not here; for he has risen, as he said. Come, see the place where he lay. Then go quickly and tell his disciples that he has risen from the dead, and behold, he is going before you to Galilee; there you will see him. Lo, I have told you.' So they departed quickly from the tomb with fear and great joy, and ran to tell his disciples.

In the Morning

O God, let me know this day the certainty shared by the
women who came first to find the stone rolled away:
    Easter day breaks!
    Christ is risen!
    Sin is conquered!

I bless you for what this glorious fact of history and faith
means to the world today:
    In times when we too know darkness and sorrow;
    In times when we too huddle bewildered amid unexpected
    happenings;
    In times when those in whom we put our hope appear to
    be defeated.

Forgive us that ever we have gone about our affairs forgetful of the triumph of Jesus, our Lord:
Trying in our own way to make sense of things;
Trying in our own strength to combat despair;
Trying to believe, apart from you, that all things will eventually come right.

I ask your special blessing this day, on all women everywhere who are faithful to Jesus Christ:
In lands newly breaking into independence;
In old lands subject to binding traditions;
In this land, sharing with me the work and witness of the Church.

I ask your special blessing this day on all women who lack the experience of Christ risen——and——
I ask your special blessing this day on all women who preach, especially——on all who teach children——on all who lead questioning youth——   AMEN

In the Evening

O God, I marvel at the worship and praise which rises to you from so many places on this day, in so many types of service, in so many languages.
I rejoice that the living Christ has transformed so many lives; and that he is adequate for whatever need any one of us may have.
Save us from vagueness that fades into unreality, and limp goodwill which achieves nothing in your eternal kingdom among men and women.   AMEN

FOURTH SUNDAY

Reading

LUKE 24: 24–29

'Some of those who were with us went to the tomb, and found it just as the women had said; but him they did not see.' And he said to them, 'O foolish men, and slow of heart to believe all that the prophets have spoken! Was it not necessary that the Christ should suffer these things and enter into his glory?' And beginning with Moses and all the prophets, he interpreted to them in all the scriptures the things concerning himself.

So they drew near to the village to which they were going. He appeared to be going further, but they constrained him, saying, 'Stay with us, for it is toward evening and the day is now far spent.' So he went in to stay with them.

In the Morning

O God, I thank you for the experiences of others, for their downcast eyes raised, their sorrowing hearts filled with joy, their tired bodies quickened to extra undertakings because of their revelation of the risen Christ.

I rejoice that he comes to us still as we walk our chosen way; that he talks with us, giving us new ideas, new approaches to the situation that bothers us; that he quickens and warms our hearts and, at our invitation, still comes in to tarry with us.

I rejoice that no home is too humble, no heart too foolish, to offer him hospitality, no moment too ordinary to receive

84

new significance, when he takes charge of it. I rejoice that he can use the shared experience of any one of us, to encourage others' faith and discipleship.

Bless all those whose faith is so real that in any situation now it refuses to be dismayed; that in days of sickness and discouragement and loneliness, knows the life-giving presence of the risen Christ; that even in the experience of death, is more than conqueror through him who loves us.

In his name, give me steady eyes, cool nerves, and a quiet heart this day.   AMEN

In the Evening

O God, I thank you for gentle healing ministries of this day:
For the gladness and freshness of the morning;
For the freedom of the wind and the sun;
For the changing beauties of skies and clouds.

I thank you for every remembrance of the past, and those who have loved you:
For those of ancient times, when life was simple;
For those who have proved steady when all about them was upset;
For those generous in service, whatever the cost to themselves.

I rejoice in the company of those who love and serve you today, especially —— and —— let your rich blessing be upon us all this night.   AMEN

FIFTH SUNDAY

Reading

JUDE 1: 21-25

Keep yourselves in the love of God; wait for the mercy of our Lord Jesus Christ unto eternal life. And convince some, who doubt; save some, by snatching them out of the fire; on some have mercy with fear, hating even the garment spotted by the flesh.

Now to him who is able to keep you from falling and to present you without blemish before the presence of his glory with rejoicing, to the only God, our Saviour through Jesus Christ our Lord, be glory, majesty, dominion, and authority, before all time and now and for ever.   AMEN

In the Morning

O God, bless this day every word, every service, every place which helps to bring us nearer to you.

Bless those who seek you in circumstances that are outwardly discouraging.

Bless those who continue loyal in service where there is none to see.

Bless those who witness to you in lands not their own, in a language not their own.

Bless those who prepare for the whole-time ministry of the Church in the world:
  Give them unquestioning devotion and love;
  Give them minds alert and flexible;
  Give them bodies strong and practical.

Bless all whose gifts of speech and pen are devoted to healing the unhappy divisions in the Church:
  Save them from superiority;
  Save them from shallow haste;
  Save them from hindering discouragement.

Bless all whose witness to the truth and spirit of the Kingdom
is expressed through politics:
Through peacemaking at high levels;
Through commerce and the concern of science;
Through homemaking and the care of little lives entrusted
to their care.
Bless especially this day, all grown grey in your service, who
care greatly for the advance of the Kingdom:
Those now frail or at a distance from church;
Those now deaf and unable to take part, as once;
Those sick, in hospital, or home.
In your mercy, meet our varied needs this day, O Lord.

AMEN

In the Evening

O Lord of Life eternal,
I bless you for the joy and refreshment of this day:
For the opportunities taken for worship;
For the certainties shared through symbol and sacrament,
sermon, and music;
For the eyes and hearts quickened through religious drama
and film;
For the minds awakened and satisfied through keen dis-
cussion;
For the steady care of those who have tended the sick and
bedfast;
For cheer brought to the aged and lonely through flowers,
books and talk.
Take all these things, done in Christ's name today, and use
them for your glory.   AMEN

SIX GRACES FOR USE AT TABLE

GRACES AT TABLE

For these good gifts, O God, we bring you our thanks—
and ourselves.   AMEN

For the food of many seasons, and the service of many
hands, accept our thanks, O Lord.   AMEN

For your unfailing care of us, we bring our thanks, O God.
Let our care of others be unfailing, too.   AMEN

Accept our thanks, O God, for all who sow and harvest,
For all who cook and serve.   AMEN

For the good food upon our table, O God,
And the good fellowship around it, we bring our thanks.
                                                            AMEN

O God, whilst you nourish our bodies,
Keep us mindful of the needs of others.   AMEN

PRAYERS WITH BIBLE READINGS
FOR FESTIVAL DAYS

CHRISTMAS DAY

In the Morning

O God, this is a wonderful morning!
The very thought of all the children I know, in the many homes I know, opening their stockings, and giving and receiving gifts, fills me with joy.

Let me not be so full of my own affairs—giving and receiving gifts, preparing meals, and perfecting decorations, that I forget the Christ-child whose birthday this is.

Let me not be so busy with my friends and family, that I spare no thought for the humble home of Nazareth, and for the homeless and the lonely ones no distance from where I am.

Widen my circle to make room for those hungry for love as much as for food; then let me spare a gift of money for the refugees, for the orphans, and victims of disaster and loss.

So let the gift of your Son, enrich all our giving and receiving this day;
And let the joy we share be as reverent and as real as that of those who came first to his manger bed.

So let this wonderful morning open out into a wonderful day, for myself and for all those I care about. To your honour and glory, now and forever.　　　　AMEN

CHRISTMAS DAY

In the Evening

With the long-loved carols and hymns and Gospel records
of the star in the sky and the child in the stall, ringing
in my heart, let me end this day.

Let me ever marvel at the coming of Christ into this world—
in a small town of your choosing, in a small country of
your choosing, to a humble couple of your choosing.

Let me ever marvel that angels and shepherds gave him
welcome, whilst the mighty in the land, and the proud
in their own secret hearts passed him by, missing one
of life's greatest moments.

Bless old and young who have opened wide their lives
to give him welcome today; bless all in the middle years
who have paused amid this day's festivities to own him
King.   AMEN

Daily Reading

LUKE 2: 11–14

For unto you is born this day in the city of David a Saviour
who is Christ the Lord. And this will be a sign for you:
you will find a babe wrapped in swaddling cloths and lying
in a manger. And suddenly there was with the angel a
multitude of the heavenly host praising God and saying,
'Glory to God in the highest, and on earth peace among
men with whom he is pleased!'

NEW YEAR'S DAY

In the Morning

O God, it is wonderful to receive this new year.

For all the happy memories of the twelve months past, I bring you my thanks. There have been so many rich moments.

There have been, too, some things I would like to forget— silly mistakes and deliberate sins. Let none of these slip from me unforgiven.

Let me step into the new year free, obedient, and eager, humble and sincere. Give me strength to complete the tasks I have undertaken.

Let my love for you and for others enrich my human relationships. Give me faith to find the best in every situation.

Give me hope, in the hour when my job seems dull, or difficult. I cannot see far, or clearly : so guide me as I go.

Let the lovely, everlasting things for which Jesus Christ lived and died and triumphed become more and more real in my life this year. For his sake.   AMEN

In the Evening

And now the day is done, O God, and the darkness gathers all living things in for rest :

And I seek rest of body, and mind, and spirit, with men and women made in your likeness.

From time beyond remembrance, others have hushed their hearts for prayer at the day's end.

Let no word cross my lips that does not come from my heart; no petition be expressed, that I do not support with my life.

Take my short-sighted requests, and strip them of self;

take my impatient requests, and answer them in your own
way, and time.

Save me from vague goodwill that evades situations that
seem difficult and forms of service that look disagreeable.

Strengthen my witness this year, in the home where I live,
in the place where I work, among those with whom I
worship.

Bless all whom I love and care about, all who make claims
upon me in any way——and——and——and——

AMEN

Daily Reading

JOHN 4: 23-30

But the hour is coming, and now is, when the true worshippers
will worship the Father in spirit and truth, for such the
Father seeks to worship him. God is spirit, and those who
worship him must worship in spirit and truth. The woman
said to him, 'I know that Messiah is coming (he who is
called Christ): when he comes, he will show us all things.'
Jesus said to her, 'I who speak to you am he.'

Just then his disciples came. They marvelled that he
was talking with a woman, but none said, 'What do you
wish?' So the woman left her water jar, and went away into
the city, and said to the people, 'Come, see a man who told
me all that I ever did. Can this be the Christ?' They went
out of the city and were coming to him.

GOOD FRIDAY

In the Morning

O God, I hush my heart before you, on this solemn day:
My thoughts fly back to that hostile crowd about my Lord,
as he staggered along, suffering at the hands of men,
bearing his cross:
My thoughts try to fathom the unplumbed depths of his
love, his shame, his loneliness;
My thoughts try to fathom the behaviour of his friends,
bewildered and afraid.

I am reassured by the faithfulness of the few who stood
by him, especially the little knot of women, with nothing
to offer but love, who went out to be with him when he
died:
My thoughts are of the passing hours and the cold indiffer-
ence or the ridicule of most;
My thoughts are of the men who gambled for his garments
and of the two wretched fellows who died beside him.

I marvel at the words which he spoke—treasured, and never
to be forgotten by those whose duty or love kept them
near enough to catch them and pass them on:
My thoughts are of his concern for the request of the
dying robber;
My thoughts are of his great cry for forgiveness for those
who knew not what they did.

I follow in imagination the loving thought of Joseph of
Arimathea, who offered his own tomb, and with it some
dignity due in death. I think of the linen and the spices:
And my thoughts can carry me no further;
And I can only bear the hurt of this hour,
As I anticipate the glory of the stone rolled away.

I can hardly wait.   AMEN

GOOD FRIDAY

In the Evening

Darkness of night seems darker, O God, for the sin of men's
    hearts that we celebrate in this hour : And
    I am as involved as the crowd then; often
    I am as divided in heart as Judas;
    I am as unreliable and impulsive as Peter;
    I am as frightened of public opinion as Pilate.
Make me, O God, as eager to minister to him as those
    faithful women, as ready to receive his loving forgiveness
    and assurance as that poor wretch to whom he promised
    paradise.   AMEN

Daily Reading

JOHN 19: 19—25

Pilate also wrote a title and put it on the cross; it read,
'Jesus of Nazareth, the King of the Jews.' Many of the
Jews read this title, for the place where Jesus was crucified
was near the city; and it was written in Hebrew, in Latin,
and in Greek. The chief priests of the Jews then said to
Pilate, 'Do not write, "The King of the Jews." ' Pilate
answered, 'What I have written I have written.'

When the soldiers had crucified Jesus they took his garments
and made four parts, one for each soldier. But the tunic
was without seam, woven from top to bottom; so they said
to one another, 'Let us not tear it, but cast lots for it to
see whose it shall be.' This was to fulfil the scripture, 'They
parted my garments among them, and for my clothing they
cast lots.'

So the soldiers did this; but standing by the cross of
Jesus were his mother, and his mother's sister, Mary the wife
of Clopas, and Mary Magdalene.

EASTER DAY

In the Morning

O Lord of Life, my heart has waited for this day as eagerly
as those women early at the tomb—to find the stone rolled
away, and no use for their spices.
O Lord of Life, I give you thanks for the Gospel records
of that great experience, made increasingly real as the
days passed.
O Lord of Life, I rejoice in the transformation of the dis-
traught and scattered disciples.
O Lord of Life, I go forth into today sharing in Christ's
triumph over sin and death:
Receive my worship and praise,
Receive my wonder and joy,
Receive my loyal and lasting allegiance.
So may thy light and life and love be abroad today in all
the dark corners of the world,
Wherever sin defies and destroys,
Wherever hopelessness deadens and dulls,
Wherever men and women are prisoners of shame and fear.
Let the triumph music and hymns of Easter day echo through
all our lives, that the things for which Christ died and
rose might be established:
Deliver us from war, and its methods;
Deliver us from racial superiority;
Deliver us from questioning your power and mighty love,
today.   AMEN

EASTER DAY

In the Evening

Deliver me, O Lord of Life, from all doubts and fears as
I hush my heart to hear echoing through all the Christian
world the words of those women who went first to the
tomb.
Let no selfish passion, or stupidity, or lowered standard of
behaviour, know victory in my life, since my Lord is risen!
Deliver me from subtle forms of self-praise, from self-trust,
from satisfaction in my own accomplishments.
Let my trust, wholly and forever, be in his risen power,
his eternal love, his mighty keeping.   AMEN

Daily Reading

LUKE 23: 55–56; 24: 1–6

The women who had come with him from Galilee followed,
and saw the tomb, and how his body was laid; then they
returned and prepared spices and ointments.

On the sabbath they rested according to the commandment.
But on the first day of the week, at early dawn, they went
to the tomb, taking the spices which they had prepared. And
they found the stone rolled away from the tomb, but when
they went in they did not find the body. While they were
perplexed about this, behold, two men stood by them in
dazzling apparel; and as they were frightened and bowed
their faces to the ground, the men said to them, 'Why do you
seek the living among the dead? Remember how he told you,
while he was still in Galilee.'

WHITSUNDAY

In the Morning

O God, let the spirit of Christ dwell in me this day:
  Saving me from sluggishness;
  Saving me from intolerance;
  Saving me from smugness.
Let this day bring to me a wonderful experience of what
  these things mean:
  Open my heart to his love;
  Open my mind to his truth;
  Open my plans to set always his will first.
And what I seek for my own life, I seek for others, especially
  ——and——and——

Banish all dullness, all dreariness, all unlovely things; and
  replace them with the joy and the vitality of Christ's spirit;
  the winsomeness of his personality; the respect and care
  he showed always for others everywhere.
Banish all superiority of colour, of race, of denomination;
  and replace them with his spirit of humility, long-suffering,
  and readiness to share. So enliven the Church we love and
  serve; and the Church in all the world.

You have made of one blood all nations to dwell together
  on the face of this earth:
  Bind us together in understanding;
  Call us to your way of peacemaking;
  Redeem us from our sins and renew us
  Today—for our hope is in his spirit.   AMEN

WHITSUNDAY

In the Evening

O God, there are so many things in this life beyond my
power to achieve, or my ability fully to understand.
Again and again, I feel my weakness and long for strength;
again and again, I feel my ignorance as a dark, cloying
thing and long for your light.
Again and again, I fail to communicate with those about
me at the deep levels of my spirit and I fall prey to dis-
couragements and doubts.
Renew in me today the living spirit of Christ and his un-
conquerable goodness and lasting joy.
Take my stupidities and my sins and in your mercy, forgive
me—and bring me to the morrow with eagerness.   AMEN

Daily Reading
GALATIANS 5: 22-26; 6: 9-10

But the fruit of the Spirit is love, joy, peace, patience, kindness, goodness, faithfulness, gentleness, self-control; against
such there is no law. And those who belong to Christ Jesus
have crucified the flesh with its passions and desires.

If we live by the Spirit, let us also walk by the Spirit.
Let us have no self-conceit, no provoking of one another, no
envy of one another. And let us not grow weary in well-
doing, for in due season we shall reap, if we do not lose
heart. So then, as we have opportunity, let us do good to
all men, and especially to those who are of the household
of faith.

ALL SAINTS DAY

In the Morning

O God, from whom all good in life comes, a glorious company of ordinary people fill my thoughts as I keep this day:
People without haloes;
People who were little praised;
People who loved you and their fellows to life's end.
O God, from whom all truth comes, I give you thanks for those who taught me to walk and to talk and to take my part:
In the affairs of school;
In the affairs of my community;
In the affairs of the Church, in your world.
O God, in whom all love begins, I bless you for those who have interpreted your values in the ordinary doings of daily life:
Filling out the riches of the mind,
Directing my feelings into healthy ways,
Widening and deepening your challenges to my dedicated will.

Whilst I owe an unpayable debt to these——to——and——and——, I bless you also for——unknown to me:
Prophets who spoke without fear;
Apostles who followed at great cost;
Martyrs and saints, all down through the centuries.
I marvel that you have called me to take my place in loving service with these, here where I am, in this century.

With the joy they knew and the courage they showed, let me live today—to your sole glory.   AMEN

ALL SAINTS DAY

In the Evening

O God, it is a wonderful thing to know that I am not called
to walk your way of life for the first time—that countless
others have chosen this way before me, with all the king-
doms of the earth in sight.

You have surrounded them with your love, and supported,
and strengthened them for what they were required to do;
so that their hearts were filled with praise, as they finished
their way here, and went on eagerly to fuller life.   AMEN

Daily Reading

HEBREWS 11: 39–40; 12: 1–2

And all these, though well attested by their faith, did not
receive what was promised, since God had foreseen something
better for us, that apart from us they should not be made
perfect.

Therefore, since we are surrounded by so great a cloud
of witnesses, let us also lay aside every weight, and sin
which clings so closely, and let us run with perseverance the
race that is set before us, looking to Jesus the pioneer and
perfecter of our faith, who for the joy that was set before
him endured the cross, despising the shame, and is seated at
the right hand of the throne of God.

THE LAST DAY OF THE YEAR

In the Morning

O God, I am full of wonder that you have brought me to
this hour.
Looking back,
Many dear people come before my mind;
Many good experiences come into focus;
Many self-centred choices seem a pity.
Forgive me for any shrinking from your holy will.
Forgive me from any discontentment with my lot.
Forgive me for any foolish and costly lack of control.

As I pass over into the new year, I would remember afresh,
and with joy:
That Jesus Christ is the same yesterday, today, and forever;
That I can enter upon no undertaking, but he is there
before me;
That no evil in heaven or earth, can bring him final defeat.

With this glorious assurance, let me go forth into life today.

AMEN

In the Evening

From the beginning of time, men and women have hesitated
at the passing of the known—and entry into the unknown.
From the beginning of time, some have laid their fears
before you, and in your wisdom, justice and mercy found
assurance.
From the beginning of time, men and women have blundered
and done foolishly, even when the way was clear; but you
have not cast them off.

For the fuller revelation of yourself in Jesus Christ, I bless
    you;
For his loving heart, his steady eyes, his practical hands,
    I bless you;
For the undimmed meaning of his life, his death, his resur-
    rection, I bless you.

Have mercy on all those who look back over this year with
    shame, especially——and——
Have mercy on all those who look back with special cause
    for thanksgiving——and——
Uphold all those whose faith is small, whose courage wavers
    ——and——
And hold us all in your mighty keeping as we go on into
    the unknown of this new year.   AMEN

Daily Reading

MATTHEW 28: 16-20

Now the eleven disciples went to Galilee, to the mountain
to which Jesus had directed them. And when they saw him
they worshipped him, but some doubted. And Jesus came
and said to them, ' All authority in heaven and on earth has
been given to me. Go therefore and make disciples of all
nations, baptizing them in the name of the Father and of the
Son and of the Holy Spirit, teaching them to observe all that
I have commanded you; *and lo, I am with you always, to the
close of the age.*'

PRAYERS
FOR SPECIAL OCCASIONS AND
PARTICULAR OCCUPATIONS

A Gardener's Prayer

O God, I bring my thanks for a little bit of your earth in which to grow things and take part in your ageless plan of life and beauty.

I find it good to know that you set the first man and woman in a garden; that you share still with those of us who care your creative joys.

I give you thanks for the feel of the soil, for the greenness of the grass, for the strength of trees, and the seemingly dead seed full of life.

I rejoice in the passing seasons—the sleep of winter, the rebirth of spring, the glory of summer, and the harvest fullness of autumn.

I marvel at the numberless forms of life—of flowers and vegetables, of grains and nuts, of grasses and weeds.

Let me be a good gardener in your service today.   AMEN

A Prayer for Animals

O God, who gives all creatures life, hear my prayer today for those denied the speech I have—all dependent on dumb appeal.

I bless you for their great diversity, especially for those able by their nature to share our human life, to depend on our care.

I rejoice in all that pets mean to little children, to the lonely, and to the aged. I pray for all living creatures in captivity.

I ask your blessing on the skill of veterinary surgeons, on all members of all societies set up to preserve the simple rights of creatures.

I ask your blessing on all working animals and on all responsible for them—that carelessness and callousness and cruelty may be done away.

I know your loving concern for these that you have created to dwell with us, because of the assurance of our Master that you mark the single sparrow's fall. In his name, I pray.   AMEN

Expecting a Baby

O God, it might seem odd to some to pray for someone not yet born—but not to you and not to me.

In these nine months of womanly patience, I have learned more than ever to marvel at your creative plans—and our part in them.

I rejoice that the fashioning of a baby, and the founding of a family, requires the gifts of body, mind and spirit you have given to us each.

Bless these days of waiting, of preparation, of tender hope. Let only things and thoughts that are clean and strong and glad be about us.

I give you thanks that from childhood till this experience of maturity, you have made it both beautiful and natural for me to give love and to receive it.

In this newest experience, hold us each safe, relaxed, and full of eager hope—even as you count each life in your presence, precious.   AMEN

A Typist's Prayer

O God, sometimes I feel I am only of small account in this office. So many things are handled, so many decisions made, that I know little about—save that I am the servant of those decisions of others.

Let me do happily and faultlessly, what I am required to do. Let me hold secure any confidential matters, any communications that come and go. Let me find interest in my work, and satisfaction, apart from my pay packet.

Let me show respect for those set above me and patience

with those who irk me. Let me be punctual, and let my
work be such that I can take a just pride in it. Let me
not waste anyone's precious time.
Bless my fellow workers and friends in this office, and all
the work they do——and——and——and——. Let both
work and play be richer for us because we have come to
know each other.   AMEN

A Teacher's Prayer

O Lord of light and truth and love, I thank you for my
place in your world family; for the training I have received;
for the work I am allowed to do.
I thank you for those from whom I have learned what I
now know; for those around me continually probing and
wondering and experimenting.
I thank you for their glorious devotion to truth and beauty
and service; for their great patience with growing minds.
I remember with thankfulness my colleagues——especially
——and——and——and——my friends——and my pupils
——and——
Inspire, inform, and support me this day.   AMEN

A Prayer Out-of-Doors

For the simple things I so often take for granted, O God,
I give you thanks now:
For the immensity of the sky,
For the fertility of the earth,
For water with reflections, dashing-smashing beauty, and
always life-giving powers;
For the song of birds,
For the natural movement of wild creatures,
For crickets and grasshoppers, and the gauzy wings of
dragonflies;
For the graceful curves of grass stalks,
For the changing colours of leaves,
For the cleansing, refreshing might of winds;

For the purity and challenge of mountain peaks,
For the awesomeness of thunder,
For the unceasing power and pull of the tides.
Above all these, I give thanks that you have placed in my
personality secrets whose issue is in eternity, power to
worship you, to love you, and to serve you now and always.
AMEN

On an Anniversary Morning

O God, I can hardly believe that the time has gone so quickly.
And here I am remembering once more, the day when first
this special happiness came to me. It doesn't seem long—
save that so much has happened.
I thank you for every supporting experience of love and
consideration. I thank you for happy surprises that have
broken in upon this year, for every tie strengthened, every
joy doubled because freely shared.
There are things I wish I hadn't to remember, some words
I wish I hadn't spoken, some thoughts I wish I hadn't
turned over in my mind, some things I wish I hadn't done.
Forgive me, I pray, and let me put behind me anything which
has marred this year together; and give me good sense and
loving strength not to do any of these things again.
Bless all those who remember this date—family, neighbours,
and friends—and share my joy. Let wonder and sincere
thanksgiving be uppermost in everything I do and say today.
AMEN

A Motorist's Prayer

O God, in a moment I shall rub up the windscreen, and
put my key into the ignition. It is wonderful to have been
born in this age.
Men and women have walked up and down this earth for
so long; men and women have travelled so slowly; men
and women have found distances so great.

III

As I get into my car, and drive off, let me do it thankfully—and responsibly. I can get so many things done in little time, because I have the car.

But let me not be tempted to speed to save a minute or two at the cost of anyone's safety, anyone's anxiety, any lack of courtesy.

Give me patience with the crippled, the aged, the slow in crossing; give me understanding of the short-sighted, the self-absorbed, the deaf.

Let me make time to keep my car in good order, that no mechanical fault I can avoid, will hold me up, or hurt or hinder another. For your love's sake.　　AMEN

Prayer of a Policewoman

O God, Creator of law and order, I walk about for hours sometimes and nobody speaks to me. But there is never a moment when I cannot speak to you or have you speak to me.

I thank you that you have full knowledge of all that goes on in this place; that you are already active in every human situation before I can get there or do a thing.

I thank you that all your purposes of justice and good neighbourliness are life-giving. Give me the judgment I need, the alertness of mind, the loving heart and the experience to help you.

Let me never forget that all day long, as in the night, I am dealing with human beings—foolish ones, lonely ones, ignorant ones, vicious ones, frustrated ones, vindictive ones —all human beings. For Christ's sake.　　AMEN

Prayer of One Newly in Hospital

O God, this day begins in a very different way from usual. I am surrounded by things I am not yet used to. I am served by people I do not yet know. I am amidst others uprooted from home, suffering in various ways.

Bless all who will do their best to help me to health and

wholeness again—doctors and nurses, lab-workers, and ward maids, and many I won't get to know at all—working to keep this place clean, to do the records, and get the meals.

Help me to be at ease with the chaplain when he comes through; to be patient and not ring my bell too often, to be cheerful when my visitors come, and to cooperate in every way I can.

Be specially close to all those I have left at home—my family, my neighbours, my friends. Be specially close to all who must do extra, because I am here—all at a distance who send me letters or flowers.

I am sure your purpose is one of loving strength and health because when Jesus was on earth he spent so much time healing, comforting, and reassuring the sick. I give myself into your keeping today and always. AMEN

A Prayer before Church

O God, bring me to church today in the right spirit. Let me rise in time to do what I must without a rush.

Bless our minister in his preparation—quicken his spirit, and clothe his message in words fresh and telling. Let the glory and greatness of the Gospel lay complete hold of him.

Bless those who have duties about the church—to support his ministry, and to make more real the worship of all of us. Bless those with whom I share my pew—especially any strangers.

Bless as truly, all those who worship you in other denominations; those who worship you in other places; those who worship you in other languages; all who are secretly seeking you outside any Church.

We are all children of your great human family—made to seek you, to know you, to love you, to serve you. AMEN

In a Time of Sadness

O God, my Father, if I couldn't come to you for comfort,
I can't think whatever I would do:

Friends are very kind—but they don't understand all that
goes to make this a sad time for me;

Members of my family are dear—but even the closest of
them, cannot fully understand.

Almost every little thing around reminds me of the past.
Lest I live on memories too much, help me.

I haven't words for what I would really like to say—but
you know how things are at the moment.

Give me something of the courage of Christ, staggering
beneath his cross and now alive for evermore.

In his living, triumphant overcoming of death, lead me
through this sad time and into greater fulness of life
and joy.

Save me from self-pity, from all that would hinder you in
your good ongoing purpose for me, and for my loved one.
For Christ's sake.   AMEN

Setting Out on a Holiday

O God, it is good to know that my holiday has really come.
I have been very tired lately. Some things I once did
without a second thought have come to be rather a burden.

Now I can catch up on my sleep—and I give thanks for
that. Now I won't need to rise at my usual hour—and
I give thanks for that. Now I shall enjoy a change of
company—and I give thanks for that.

Let me not forget those who are still at work about me,
some of them tired too. Let me be considerate in accepting
their services. Let me be cheerful and thoughtful for those
on holiday with me.

Quicken all our senses, that new beauties of sight and sound
do not pass unnoticed; let us find delight in simple things;
let laughter stand tiptoe, ready to be of our company at
any time.

May every still lake mirror your peace; every lapping tide

speak your message to our hearts; every tiny wind minister refreshment; every star overhead in the velvety darkness spell out your steadfastness. So bless our going out and our coming in. AMEN

A Speaker's Prayer

O God, source of life and truth and loveliness, soon I must stand before your people. Clear my mind, quicken my memory, enable me to be:
Thorough in my preparation;
Make me responsive to your guidance;
Able to judge what will be most worthwhile;
Take away my natural fears and hesitancies.
Let me wear the right clothes and hat, that I may the better forget myself. Let me speak clearly and naturally, that listening will be pleasant and that the deaf may hear.
Let me keep to my point and not forget how time passes. Let me not try to be clever or lose the human touch, and let me find a natural chink for a lightsome chuckle.
And when it is over, save me from being unduly puffed-up if it has gone well, or from being too miserable if it was not as good as sometimes—if one of my best points went astray, or couldn't be heard when the baby cried or the old lady coughed.
I am your servant—still eager to serve, still ready to learn. For Christ's sake. AMEN

Prayer of a Woman Living Alone

O God, I live alone like many in this city, this country. I do my own work, I go in and out, I think my own thoughts.
I am friendly to those I know, but nobody knows me as you do,
And nobody anywhere is so close and so understanding.
Bless all those I know who live alone from choice,
All who live alone following a death,

All who live alone because of estrangement,
All who live alone for financial reasons.
Bless each small room I think of, each flat, each too large old house,
Wherever one raises her voice to you in prayer at any time.
Bless especially, any one of us who has grown shy, selfish, or odd,
Anyone who would like to change, but feels she can't; anyone ill, or frail.
Some of us are young still and we enjoy freedom,
We go out and we come in—we visit and have visitors;
We are happy to surround ourselves with beauty;
We enjoy our meals and flowers and pretty things.
Single, married, divorced—young, middle-aged, old—we are all your children, part of your great human family. All the time, we need courage and reassurance and your loving care and presence. Keep us.   AMEN

Prayer before a Routine Job

O God, this must be done though it's dull.
Give me the courage to begin and to put it off no longer;
And give me perseverance to complete it.
I am glad that no line can be drawn between things— what we call ' sacred ', and what we call ' secular ',
What we do once in a while, or have to do continually, is important to you.
Accept the skill within my hands, today,
Give me good judgment and patience.
Forgive me, if I've been lazy about starting this job.
Let me find pleasure in things beautiful, and good and true.   AMEN

Prayer of a Waitress

O God, you made men and women to hunger and thirst and to need rest and refreshment and talk together. It is not always easy to remember these things when the place is full, with more coming all the time.

Sometimes when there is a rush, it takes me all my time to be patient. People are very demanding, and their disappointment when I can't supply their requests is sometimes shown in an unkindly way.

I am thankful for those who are a joy to serve—who are so courteous always, so pleasant. You know how these things help when I have been on my feet for hours and must keep going.

I don't have any chance to think about the Feeding of the Five Thousand when I'm at work—I haven't the time. But when I can, I am thankful that Jesus knows what hungry people are.

It helps me too, to remember whenever I can that he knows what tiredness is. He sat once on a well-side to rest when most others were free to enjoy their midday siesta out of the heat.

It helps me to remember, even when my feet are aching and my back seems ready to break, that I can serve him by offering in his name even a cup of cold water. I remember then that all my customers are your people.

This isn't much of a prayer—but you know what I mean. I offer it, in Christ's name.   AMEN

Prayer of a Shop Assistant

You know how it is, O God—sometimes I'm rushed, sometimes there is very little doing. I'd sooner be busy—to hang around is irksome. The time drags then, when I've tidied up my drawers and stands.

I don't think about him much at work, but of course Jesus handled goods and money and served people in his little business at Nazareth. So he knows what it takes to be patient with those who waste my time.

May his courtesy, that shines through the New Testament record of his dealings with people always, be mine today. Let me enjoy my job—and use well and responsibly the wage I earn. For his name's sake.   AMEN

A Prayer before the Fire

O God, nobody is around just now. And it is lovely to sit here a few minutes quietly and alone. I know that, in the most wonderful sense, I am never alone—always your living presence is with me. And it is true now.

So many things have filled the day, so many others have made claims upon me, that it is not possible to keep awareness of you in the front of my thoughts all the time. And yet life would be impossible, if it were not true.

As I hush my heart before you things sort themselves out. Some things of little importance have crowded into the day—some, that I count important, have been given a place. I am not always able to decide which is which in your eyes.

Nobody could have known, without help, how important a cup of cold water given in Christ's name might be; nobody could have guessed that the lint-bandage of the Good Samaritan, and his oil and twopence would serve you so lastingly.

Help me in my relationships with those dear ones with whom I shall shortly share this fire, kindled so warmly, in the simplest things, and the commonest. Let me serve you, in serving and loving them. For Christ's sake.

AMEN

Entering upon Retirement

O God, my life has been a busy one. Retirement has seemed a long way off—and now it is here.

One day seems much like another at the moment. It is odd to be able to choose my task, and my time.

I give you thanks for all my fellow workers whose faces crowd into my vision as I think of them——and——

I give you thanks for skills learned, experiences shared, and some satisfaction in having done my best.

Now that I shall be much more about the home, make me easy to plan with, quick to give praise and slow to offer criticism before being asked.

Now that I shall have time for hobbies and new interests, let me discover new friendships, new enthusiasms, new ways of giving a helping hand.

Enable me to live at peace with my inmost self, with those with whom my days are cast, and with you—that rid of many pressures of working, earning and spending, life may be good. AMEN

A Student's Prayer

O God, it is good to be alive and here—though it's hard to wait to do all the things I want to do.

You have made the world so rich, so great, so crammed full of possibilities. You have made it so beautiful.

I thank you for all who have given me this chance to learn, and to get ready for life; my family, my teachers, my friends.

Let me show a proper reverence for things that have come to me at cost of others' toil, even tears. My heritage as a woman is rich.

Establish my values—and let my body, mind and spirit have part only in that which is clean and good and joyous.

In moments of temptation, let me not lower my standards, but depending on your strength, given to many another before me, win through.

Enrich my friendships here, enrich my fun, and give me a lively concern for the lot of less fortunate women in other countries.

Widen my horizon, widen my sympathies, and when I am finished here, let me give myself to serve your ongoing purposes in this wonderful world. AMEN

When Caring for One Sick at Home

O God, just now the routine has to be changed. Let me be wise in deciding what is best to do.

Match my concern with loving care, my sympathy with good sense, my patience with cheerfulness.

Let me be self-forgetful, ready to interpret the doctor's
orders in the most helpful way.

Give me loving respect for——'s body; let me think of
interesting things to engage a tired mind.

When the telephone rings, let me answer wisely and kindly
the enquiries of others who care.

Let flowers and books and beautiful surroundings have my
concern, as well as comfortable pillows.

Help me to think of tempting meals, and to prepare nice
trays.

So I may serve your purpose of wholeness and health and
joy. Through Jesus, the great physician.   AMEN

Approaching Spring Cleaning

O God, you know how many things I have put off doing.
The days have been so full. And I have been a bit lazy
about tackling this job.

Save me from making excuses for myself, that I am not
as ready to make for others. And give me courage to rid
my house of all shabby, useless things.

Let my duster reveal hidden beauties and my bonfire bring
you praise as it gives me joy. Let me live and serve you
in sweet orderliness.

And let me as thoroughly rid my mind and heart of all
shabby prejudices, and unkind judgments, and tangles of
self-pity, of all untrue ideas.

So straighten out my sense of values—that my cupboards
and drawers and shining surfaces may praise you; and
my body, mind and spirit bring you glory.   AMEN

Before Shopping for Clothes

It is wonderful, O God, to know that you care how the
hills are clothed and how the trees, birds and living
creatures are made ready for life.

I often notice the coats of cats and dogs, the feathers of

common sparrows counted of little worth and the fins of fish.

I notice the coats of horses and cows and goats, and those or others unfamiliar save in the zoo—elephants, giraffes, donkeys, tigers, polar bears.

To each of these, and countless others, you have given what best suits its habitat, and nature of life. Each is so fittingly clothed.

Let me find, out of all that the shops offer, what best suits my way of life. Give me good judgment, and taste. Save me from coveting what I can't afford.

Save me from falling for a fashion that doesn't suit me. Give me patience to keep on looking if at first I don't find the right thing.

Let my bodily clothing concern me no more than the clothing of my heart and mind. Let me be beautiful within— with sincerity, faith, joy, love, gladness of your choicest making.   AMEN

A Prayer for the Right Use of Words

O God, women have been charged with being chatterboxes since the beginning of time. Sometimes it has been deserved. Sometimes our words have led us into trivial judgments, into unkindly gossip.

But I bless you for this wonderful means of communication with others about us—others wiser than we are, others dependent on us, others more mature in the things of the spirit, others sharing good news.

I rejoice in all who use words to speak where many listen, to write what many read, to broadcast to those they may never meet, to present dramatic acts full of meaning and stimulus.

I share responsibility for the right use of words with many other women—in cities and the country's quiet places— who serve as journalists, reporters, and authors, in publishing houses and in bookshops.

I think especially just now, of——and——

Let me never at any time write or say in a book, a paper,

a letter, or in chance conversation, anything for which anyone will be sorry afterwards.

Let me never pander to standards of poor taste; let me never tell a lie about another, even to entertain; let me never stoop to subtle forms of self-praise.

Let the thoughts of my mind, and the words on my lips be strong, clear, and life-giving. Enable me to use them skilfully, interestingly, beautifully.

I ask this in the name of Christ, the true Word of Life.

AMEN

Confession after a Quarrel

O God, I need your forgiveness. I've been stupid again. I have sinned against your commandment to love with all my heart and mind and soul and to love others as I love myself.

Forgive me, and help me to forgive as freely.
If it wasn't wholly my fault, I am much to blame.
Keep me from foolish pride likely to prolong this unhappy state of affairs.
And give me grace at once to make the first move in putting things right between us. AMEN

Prayer of One Bedfast

Gracious Father, each day isn't very different from the one before it in some ways. I can't take any active part in the bustle of the big world:

And yet every day brings some small reminder of your loving care, shown through family and friends, through letters from afar, through flowers.

My body holds me here, but my mind and spirit can circle the earth. I thank you for this. I can hold up before you in loving prayer all for whom I care.

I can read a little if the print is good: I thank you for

this. I can listen to the wireless a little and watch television for a while before tiring.

My visitors bring me news, and my doctor comes in and out, encouraging me and tending me; my minister remembers me and this room becomes my chapel.

Keep me in your love; save me from self-pity; let me be endlessly appreciative of those who help me so much; save me from being a burden to them.　　AMEN

A Prayer of a Young Mother

O God, I hardly have a moment to myself. As I get my husband off, and the children bathed and clad and fed, the phone rings, or a neighbour calls.

I can't always do what I would like to do about the house: there is the endless washing for the children—when the weather allows—and the airing.

I have the shopping to do and I take the littles ones with me for an outing—and the hours fly. In no time I'm putting them to rest and planning the meal.

Help me to make this house a home, full of joy and security; a home to which we will all be eager to return at the day's end, a centre of understanding and love.

Help me to make time for the most important things; and not to become so overtired that I forget that you have honoured me with this far-reaching, and rewarding task.

Bless our free times together—all our fun; bless our plans, as we look ahead; our relationships with friends in the community, and in the church here, and in the wide world. For your Kingdom's sake.　　AMEN

A Nurse's Prayer

O God, my Father, I offer to you the love of my heart, the skills that reside in my hands and the strength of my body, this day.

Let the compassion of Jesus as he moved amongst the sick,

ministering to the pain-wracked, the mentally distraught, and the frightened, be mine.

When every bed in the ward is full and the bell keeps ringing and emergencies occur, keep me unflustered.

Grant me gentleness always, cheerfulness, and the power to match firmness with persuasion. So let me minister your gift of wholeness to those in my charge.   AMEN

A Missionary's Prayer

Rising time comes early here. Let my first thoughts be offered to you, O God, as I waken.

I thank you that in a way unmistakable, your call to this service came to me:

I owe a debt to many who have helped to
Train me,
Send me,
Support me.

I have blundered occasionally, for all
My care,
My love of these people,
My faith in the worthwhileness of it all.

I have prayed that others might come to help:
With youthful energies,
With still better qualifications,
With joyous devotion that asks only to give.

Bless my colleagues this day, and all here and at home, who hold me in their love—and in yours—through prayer.

Strengthen my body, when work and climate prove taxing; support my spirit when during days of giving out, I find so little time in which to take in.

So let my life be well spent, my faith be deepened, and my experience of your almighty power be enriched.

So continue to bless my going out and my coming in.

                                                   AMEN

Prayer on a Marriage Morning

O God, it is wonderful to waken up this morning—to share this day for which we have waited so eagerly.

I thank you for your sweet and mysterious gift of love—for all that we find in each other that attracts and enriches.

Make our relationship begun in your presence—gladdened by family and friends gathered this day within the church—strong, holy, and deathless.

Bless the home that we plan and build and keep together. Let its door be ever open to things true and beautiful and joyous.

Let us so love and trust you in the light that if dark skies are ever above us, we shall know how near you are, how loving, and how dependable.

In the name of Jesus, our Lord and Master, who began his public ministry among people at a young couple's marriage feast in Cana—I fashion this simple prayer.   AMEN

A Social Worker's Prayer

O God, I am so glad that you have called me to work with people rather than with things:
They are your people, though they lay claims upon me;
They are your people, though they are often self-willed and foolish;
They are your people, though they bring suffering upon themselves, and upon others.

O God, I am grateful for my training, and for my colleagues who support me day by day: but
Every human situation presents new factors,
Every individual in trouble calls for a fresh concern.

O God, take my whole personality—body, mind and spirit, and work through me:
Deliver me from condemnation,
From arrogance, and intolerance,
From impatience.

O God, love these people, one by one, into new beginnings, and better life:

Meet them with sympathy always,
With gentleness when they need it,
With sternness when that can best serve.
For Christ's sake. AMEN

A Prayer on Opening My Bible

As I settle for this time of quiet, O God, hush my heart
and quicken my understanding.
I bless you for scribes, scholars and translators who have
served your holy will.
I bless you for the great Bible Societies that have made this
book available in my language.
I pray for a living expectancy, as I wait to learn what you
will say to me while I read.
I pray for courage to face new challenges and to embrace
new truth. For Christ's sake. AMEN

A Prayer on Starting a New Book

O God of many voices, all truth is yours.

I thank you for the power to read, to discriminate and to
enjoy.
I thank you for authors of books who dedicate their skills
to you.
I thank you for librarians and booksellers who foster the best.

For every glimpse of beauty, I bless you; for every new
truth that has beckoned me out beyond the place I have
trod so often and the opinion I have held so long.
AMEN

A Musician's Prayer

O God, it is beyond my powers to think what this world
would be without music.

I bless you for the special sounds of birds, of streams, and
winds, and mighty seas.

I bless you for nursery lullabies and folk songs and the
early musical delights of youth.

I bless you for music, deep and moving, which says to
human hearts in sorrow or joy what words cannot say.

I bless you for the countless occasions when music has led
me out of weakness into strength, out of pettiness into
greatness of spirit.   AMEN

A Birthday Prayer

O God, I want my word to be one of praise to you as I
open my eyes on this special day.

So many good things have come into my life this year——
and——and——

I give thanks
  As I remember them one by one,
  As I remember my family——
  As I remember old friends——
I give thanks, that you have brought new people
  Into my home life——
  Into my work life——
  Into my Church life——
I give thanks that in some undertakings I have
  Known the sweet reward of success;
  Known the breaking of light in doubt;
  Known the discipline of disappointment.
I give thanks for all the beautiful things——
  The changing face of earth and sky;
  The delight of living creatures;
  The confidence of little children.

I give thanks for hilarious moments,
    Shared in books and papers;
    Shared by friends;
    Shared unconsciously by humourless people, and pompous.

I give thanks for all that has come into my life through
    my reading of Scripture, my worshipping with others,
    my service offered, my money given, for your name's sake.

I give thanks for all that has ministered to my deeper under-
    standing, my practical usefulness, my maturity—involve-
    ment in others' suffering, and loss, and renewal, for your
    name's sake.

I give thanks that all 'my joy is touched with pain', that
    the Cross of Jesus stands at the heart of this universe,
    leading on to the unbelievable miracle of death's stone
    rolled away, for your name's sake.

Forgive me for the faith I lacked;
Forgive me for the chances I failed to take;
Forgive me for the money I gave, only to hide what I
    withheld.

Make this day a happy day,
    For you,
    For myself, and
    For everybody who knows it is my birthday.   AMEN